The Devil and the Lady

AND

Unpublished Early Poems

The Devil and the Lady

AND

Unpublished Early Poems

BY

Alfred Tennyson

EDITED BY CHARLES TENNYSON

HIS GRANDSON

1964

INDIANA UNIVERSITY PRESS

BLOOMINGTON

Introduction to New Edition

In 1930 and 1931 Sir Charles Tennyson published, from manuscripts in his possession, two volumes of previously unknown works by his grandfather, the laureate. The value of these slim books, *The Devil and the Lady* and *Unpublished Early Poems*, was instantly recognized. The *Times* reviewer called *The Devil* . . . "astonishingly mature" and "of high value . . . as a biographical document" (January 30, 1930). *Unpublished Early Poems* was characterized a year later as follows:

> All these things, not first-rate in themselves, are well worth rescuing now for the abundant promise they show. Taken altogether they are in fact, despite their imperfections, more promising than much of the more finished work on the strength of which youth is wont to come forward publicly as a candidate for the laurel. The boyish pieces show deeper thoughts than those of boyhood.   (*Times Literary Supplement*, December 10, 1931)

These two volumes were brought out in limited editions of fifteen hundred each and soon were virtually unobtainable. Many a major library does not possess both and the occasional copy which comes up for sale brings the price of a rare book. It is particularly important that these poems are once again brought to the attention of the public, now that serious interest in Tennyson is more a tradition than a revival.

These poems are of especial value to the modern scholar because they seem to be the only substantial Tennyson juvenilia which will be allowed to meet the light of day. Tennyson preserved his manuscripts rather carefully and he disposed of very few in his lifetime. One notable exception is the early manuscript of *In Memoriam* which Tennyson gave to Sir John Simeon and which Lady Simeon subsequently presented, with extremely unwieldy restrictions on its use, to the library of Trinity College, Cambridge. The bulk of the material was, however, left to Tennyson's son and biographer, Hallam. Toward the end of his life Hallam, Lord Tennyson, gave many of these original manuscripts to British university libraries. The manuscript of "Gareth and Lynette" went to the Bodleian Library at Oxford; others were presented to the Cambridge University Library, but the bulk joined the *In Memoriam* manuscript at Trinity. All of these donations were made with unusual declarations of gift. Lord Tennyson wished that "the fullest use" should be made of the manuscripts for exhibition purposes, but that they should not be used to produce a variorum edition of Tennyson's works, nor should they be published. Strange though these restrictions are, they are less stringent than the terms of gift for *In Memoriam*. Because of the peculiar conflict in the donor's wishes, the Bodleian Library has recently seen fit to relax the restrictions under which they previously held the Tennyson literary remains. These holdings are interesting indeed but do not contain previously unpublished works. A number of highly interesting poems which have never been published are, however, contained in the manuscripts which are kept by Trinity College. Unhappily, the College Council of Trinity and the Syndics of the Cambridge University Library have not seen fit to follow the lead of the Bodleian and, perforce, these poems must remain unknown to the public.

Fortunately for our knowledge of Tennyson's poetry, Hallam Tennyson did not leave all his holdings with such difficult restrictions. He bequeathed a goodly number to his nephew, Charles (now Sir Charles) Tennyson, and others to his son Lionel, third Baron. *Unpublished Early Poems* was edited, therefore, from manuscripts which remained in the family after the death of Tennyson's son. *The Devil and the Lady* was edited from a copy of the Trinity MS. (o.15.19), a copy made, needless to say, before the donation. These family manuscripts, some of which are now in the Houghton Library, Harvard, and some of which are now placed in the Tennyson Research Centre, Lincoln, and Hallam Tennyson's gifts to the Bodleian Library, must remain the chief public sources of information about Tennyson's work. These manuscripts may yet prove to contain a few additional fragments worthy of publication, but the most important collection of juvenilia will always be the one which Sir Charles presents again at this time.

The present volume is a facsimile reproduction of the texts and illustrations of the two original editions.

ROWLAND L. COLLINS

Indiana University

THE DEVIL AND THE LADY

Martha

Mar

TRANSLATION
of
CLAUDIAN'S

Proserpine

by A. Tennyson

JUVENTUTEQ

SPES ALIT

ET POESIN

VETUPERATIO ET PREMIT

LÆDIT

A. Tennyson

INTRODUCTION

MY UNCLE, HALLAM, LORD TENNYSON (who was the poet's son, and died in December, 1928), when he gave the most complete MS. of this play to Trinity College, Cambridge, had a copy made of it, which he left to me with other manuscripts of his father's poems, giving me leave to publish at my discretion. With this copy he wrote the following preface:—

"I have published 'The Devil and the Lady' because of the note in my Grandfather, Dr. Tennyson's handwriting to the effect that the comedy was composed by my father at the early age of 14.* He thought that it showed evidence of a wide range of reading, a power of drawing character, and an extraordinary variety of knowledge on many subjects remarkable in a youth of that age. It has been thought that this work, as a literary curiosity, might well be given to the World, not only for the benefit of students of my father's poems, but also for a wider public."

My Uncle did not, in fact, publish the play, although he included in his Memoir of the poet (see "Tennyson—a Memoir," Vol. I. pp. 25 and 26) a short quotation from it.

* This note is on the Trinity MS.— ED.

I know, however, that publication was often in his mind and that, in issuing this volume, I am not acting against his wishes.

To anyone who reads the play it must seem an almost incredible achievement for a boy of 14. But though Dr. Tennyson's statement is astonishing, I do not think that there can be any doubt of its substantial accuracy. It is confirmed by the poet himself in a statement quoted in the Memoir (vol. 1, p. 12), and clearly referring to this play. Moreover, the manuscript evidence suggests that the first version of the play at least was composed by the poet at the age stated by his father, though it may have been revised and added to during the succeeding year or two years.

The Trinity manuscript is not all in the poet's writing, the greater part of it being written in a hand which I cannot identify. There is, however, another manuscript (in my possession) which is all in Tennyson's own hand. It is contained in a small, brown-covered notebook, measuring about $5\frac{1}{2}$ inches by 3 inches, with a number of other early poems and fragments, and is clearly an earlier draft than the Cambridge manuscript, since many passages of importance are added in the latter, and some of them are written out roughly on isolated pages of the note-book, evidently as the result of a revision of the first draft, and (judging by the handwriting) immediately after its completion. Amongst other differences, the name of the Lady in the first draft is "Jessica," while in the later version it has been changed to the much less hackneyed and more suitable "Amoret."

The title-page of the notebook and a typical page of the MS. are reproduced on the frontispiece and facing p. 44 of this volume, and the two make a curious contrast, the title-page being an essentially schoolboyish production with its sprawling handwriting and scribbled drawings, while the actual play is exquisitely written in a hand wonderfully formed for a boy of 14 and remarkably like that of the poet in later life, though more upright.

This book contains another curious foretaste of the mature Tennyson in the Latin sentence written on the title-page—"*Spes alit juventutem et poesin, vituperatio premit et laedit*" (Hope nourishes youth and poesy, abuse represses and injures it).* One sees here, already shadowing his boyish mind, that extravagant sensibility to criticism which he was never able to shake off even at the zenith of his fame, and which after the critical *vituperatio* of 1833 kept him silent

---

* This may be a quotation, but I have not been able to identify it.—ED.

for what should have been nine of the most fruitful years of his life.

My Uncle in his Memoir states that this play and certain other poems which he there quotes, were omitted from the "Poems by Two Brothers" (published in 1827) as being too much out of the common for the public taste. Drafts and fragments of some of Tennyson's contributions to the "Two Brothers" volume are included in the notebook, *e.g.* the first three stanzas of the ode "Jerusalem" (p. 145 of the "Poems by Two Brothers," reprint of 1896) and "The Sun goes down in the Dark Blue Main" (*ib.* p. 157). There are also about 150 lines from a translation of Claudian's "Proserpine" (mentioned on the title-page—see frontispiece) into the regular Popeian metre, in which, according to the poet's own statement, he composed hundreds of lines, after reading Pope's "Homer" at the age of 10 and 11. Tennyson himself stated that his contributions to the "Poems by Two Brothers" were written between the ages of 15 and 17, and these are evidently all very early poems, since ink and handwriting correspond exactly with the draft of the play in the same book.

The Trinity manuscript, which is contained in a notebook of similar size and binding, is evidently a copy, made mostly by another hand, from this first draft, and the poet afterwards worked on the second draft, since many passages are added by his hand, some interpolated in the text and some written on the blank pages alongside of the text, while the last few pages (about one-fifth of the whole) are all in his writing. These added passages seem to be in a later hand than that of the first draft. The ink is blacker and the writing freer, more sloping and more like the poet's mature hand. I do not think, however, judging from the other contents of the Trinity volume and from a comparison with other early manuscripts, that any of these passages are likely to have been written after the poet was 16, and one or two are revisions of added passages in the earlier notebook. It is remarkable that many of the best passages occur in the first draft, though the later additions contain the more characteristically Tennysonian passages.

I have described the contents of these early MS. books somewhat minutely, partly because they seem indirectly to support the statement as to the writer's age, and partly because I think that these early unpublished writings should help to correct a false impression which has been created by criticisms of the "Poems by Two Brothers." Critics, such as Andrew Lang and

Stopford Brooke, have claimed that Tennyson's contributions to this volume show no sign of the originality and force which marked even the volume of 1830 (published only three years later) and, much more strongly, that of 1833. Such criticism seems to suggest some sudden and unexplained development of the poet's mind between the dates of the earlier and later publications. The true explanation of this apparent discrepancy is given in the statement already quoted from the Memoir, that this play and certain other poems were deliberately omitted from the "Poems by Two Brothers" as being too much out of the common for the public taste. Jowett, who was consulted by the poet's son about these omitted poems, said that they were most original and that it was wonderful how the whelp could have known such things. The Master was apparently, consciously or unconsciously, adapting Doctor Johnson's well-known saying about another "Marvellous Boy," the unhappy Chatterton, but the words fit well enough where he applied them, and it must, I think, be plain to anyone who reads this play with the other boyish poems quoted in the Memoir, that Tennyson was, even at the early age of 14, in addition, of course, to much that was imitative and second-hand, already writing highly original and characteristic verse.

A boy must naturally found his earliest work on the models which he has studied, and the study of the Elizabethans is evident in this play,* but the freedom and vivacity of the adaptation are remarkable, while every now and then there are lines which clearly foreshadow the powers of observation and intensely personal utterance which the poet developed in his maturity. For example,

" Like the low hum of the delighted bee
    In the calyx of a lily."
            .   .   .
" The mirror of the silver lake
    In its clear picture deftly pencilling
    The soft inversion of the tremulous woods."
            .   .   .
            " Each hoar wave
    With crisped undulation arching rose,
    Thence falling in white ridge with sinuous slope
    Dash'd headlong to the shore and spread along
    The sands its tender fringe of creamy spray."
            .   .   .
" There came a band of melancholy sprites
    White as their shrouds, and motionlessly pale,
    Like some young ashwood, when the argent moon
    Looks in upon its many silver stems."

* My grandfather seems to have written another play at the same time and in the same manner (see quotation in the Memoir, Vol. I. p. 23), but I have been unable to trace the manuscript, which I fear must have been destroyed.—ED.

But it is not only in occasional lines and passages that the play is characteristic and individual. Imitative though it may be, it breathes throughout a delightful freshness and freedom. In its exuberance of language, its crude schoolboy humour, the vivacity of its character drawing, its boyishly passionate aspiration, so urgent that it often finds utterance through the mouth of the Devil himself, it seems to me to stand most firmly on its own base, a living and personal thing.

The poet's own shrinking from publicity, his deliberate suppression of the personal note and the destruction of early records, such as the correspondence with Arthur Hallam, have made it difficult for later generations to realise the extraordinary force and charm of that many-sided personality which, from his first appearance at Cambridge, won for Tennyson the affectionate and delighted admiration of all with whom he came into intimate contact. This play, in its unguarded freshness, shows us Tennyson the boy, and should help not a little to solve the enigma of Tennyson the man.

Except for some minor changes in punctuation, necessitated by the writer's extraordinary fondness for dashes, and the restoration of one or two words from the earlier manuscript to repair obvious mistakes, I have printed the play from the retained copy of the Trinity manuscript exactly as Tennyson left it. He never brought it to an end, and there is no record of the way in which he intended to end it. Moreover, in revising he sometimes left loose ends and unfinished lines. No attempt has been made to correct these defects. Nor have I made any effort to trace literary parallels or references, the few notes which I have added being merely intended to make intelligible words and phrases which might otherwise have been obscure to the ordinary reader.

C. T.

DRAMATIS PERSONAE

MAGUS A Necromancer

AMORET His Wife

ANTONIO A Lawyer

PHARMACEUTUS An Apothecary

STEPHANIO A Sailor

ANGULO An Astronomer and Mathematician

CAMPANO A Soldier

BENEDICT A Monk

DEVIL *****

ACT 1

MAGUS Now doth the vollied and rebellowing thunder
Rock the huge earth, and all the dizzy hills
Quake at his coming, while the arrowy bolt
With ravaging course athwart the dark immense
Comes rushing on its wings of fire—the North
With hoarse congratulation and wild threats
Gives answer to his brother winds that rave
From the three corners of the lurid sky.
The spirits of past time are on the blast,
They leave their misty halls to commune with
The airy footed children of the storm—
Dimly they ride in gleaming steel upon
The vaultings of their cloudy chariots—
O thou omnipotent Love, whose boundless sway
And uncontroll'd dominion boweth down
The Spirits of the Mighty, thou great Despot,
Who bindest in thy golden chains the strong
And the imbecile, thou immortal Pan-Arch
Tyrant o' th' earth and sea whose sunless depth
And desolate Abyss is vivified
And quicken'd at thy bidding—thou vast link
Of the Creation—thou deep sentiment!
Thou only to be understood by those
Who feel thee and aid thy purpose, albeit I
    summon
Into thy presence Beings whose dark brows
Are furrow'd with the care of pride, whose natures

B   I

Hold less congeniality with thine
Than the condensèd, cold compacted wave
To a consuming fire—But to my task!

[*He draws a cabalistic ring on the ground*

'Tis well! Mishapen imp,
Last born of triform Hecate, hear my voice!
Stand forth and wait my summons, Spirit of Hell!

[D E V I L *starts up in the middle of the ring*

All hail! All hail! thou solitary power
Whose habitation is the grisly flame
Which guards that gate of Hell that looks along
The measureless deep, whose inky waste divides
The Evil and the Blest—Now weave thy web
Of subtle machination, ply thy power
In such a delicate and important cause
As needs thy chief attention—mark me well!

D E V I L I come, O I come, at the sound of my name
From the depths and the caverns of Hell where I
    lie,
I can rush through the torrent and ride on the
    flame
Or mount on the whirlwind that sweeps thro' the
    sky—
What wilt thou have me do for thee? Shall I weave
The sunbeams to a crown for thy bald brows?
Shall I ungarter the Plëiades for thee
And twist their glittering *periscelides**
To keep the hose up on thy minishing calves?
Shall I unchair Cassiopeia's brightness
And fetch her close stool for thee? or pluck the
    Nanny-goat

* Greek word meaning "garters."—ED.

2

From off the back of that old blade whose haunches
Quiver beneath the feather'd foot of Perseus?*
Shall I ungird Orion's strength, or bring thee
A grinder of that mighty snake, whose folds
Far stretching through the unconfined space
Involve seven worlds?

MAGUS   A truce with thine heroics!
A murrain take thine ill tim'd pleasantry!
If thou are not the most impertinent Devil
That ever smelt bitumen, pri'thee hear me.
Affairs of high importance call me hence,
Nor would I borrow of that usurer
Procrastination, whose vast interest
Is almost higher than his principal.
Procrastination, like the wayward tide,
With imperceptible and secret course
Gains hourly on us till that we are left
No landing place whereon to set our feet—
So lost and tangled is the maze of cares
Protracted and put off from day to day.

DEVIL What is the end and purport of thy words?
And wherewith can I serve thee?

MAGUS   Thou shalt hear:
For I forthwith upon the yeasty wave,
With hasty expedition of swift oars
Shall now embark—but to thee I commit
(Until such time as I retrace my way)

* This refers to the constellation Auriga, which is shown
on old astronomical maps as an old man seated with a goat
on his left arm, the constellation Perseus, which is next to
Auriga on the right, being shown as a standing figure of the
hero facing towards Auriga with the right foot raised.—ED.

3

My loving wife, to guard her chaste and pure
As stainless snow, brush'd by the windy wing
Of Eagle on the stormy mountain top,
Or like the virgin lily, whose rare sweets
Combining with the ambient atmosphere,
Do make a paradise of this fair earth,
So delicate are its odours.

DEVIL   Gentle master,
I would do ought but this—I'd dive i' th' sea,
I'd ride the chariot of the rocking winds
Alarum'd by the thunder's awful knell,
Or from the hornéd corners of the Moon
I'd pluck the charméd flowers that flourish there;
I'd visit far Arcturus, the bright length
Of the Ecliptic and the spangled Lyre,
Or that dim star which in Boötes' wain
Shines nightly, or I'd bring thee gems from out
The stilly chambers of the mighty deep,
The boundless halls of porphyry, where sit
The ancient fathers of the sea with beards
That sweep the burnish'd chrysolite beneath 'em—
All this and more I'd do for thee, for these
Are trifles to that weighty task, to guard
A woman 'gainst her will.

MAGUS   This once, good Friend,
Exert thy power—the task is short—eftsoones
I shall be here again—till then farewell!

[*Exit* MAGUS.

4

Scene II

DEVIL A very decent, tolerable task—
    Outwit a woman—that were difficult;
    Place in one scale my graceless Devilship—
    Her ladyship in t'other—weigh us both,
    I do much fear me lest her ladyship
    Untwist my meshes, foil my purposes
    And by her subtile intricacy of wit
    Mislead my choicest, noblest, nicest guile.
    The very fuscous and embrownéd cheek
    Of his Satanick Majesty might blanch
    Before a woman's art. O Styx and Acheron!
    What deprecations, amulets and charms,
    What exorcisms, crossings and bead countings,
    What Ave-Maries will be play'd against me!
    I value not your amulets and charms
    The twentieth part of half a rotten murphy
    Or a split pea, albeit I do confess me
    I'm apt to turn tail on an Ave-Mary,
    And quail a little at a Pater-Noster,
    Except when it's said backwards. I remember me
    When I was summon'd up by this same Magus
    And unto this same office ('twas the dead
    Of a most chilly winter) that I lit
    I' th' grey o' th' morning on a blue nos'd Monk
    And pluck'd him by the beard, whereat he shrunk
    In all his sinews like a sensitive plant
    And chatter'd from the bottom of his cowl
    " *Apage Sathanas iniquissime!* "
    Whereat I tripp'd him up and laid him prone
    Holding close conference with his Mother Earth
    About the damage of his splinter'd nose,

And having punch'd him fundamentally
With my strong hooves, I left him bruised and
  battered
As a beefsteak.

SCENE III

MAGUS There is nothing on all this earth that's preci-
  ous
To him who owns it, but Anxiety,
With heavy Anthesis i' the other scale,
O'er balances the pleasure on't: the rich ore
Is mixed with so much dross we cannot separate it.
There gleams no blue speck in the clouded waste
Of the charg'd atmosphere (not more perchance
Than is enough to make a butcher's surtout)
But minute after minute threatens us,
Lest in the misty wrappings of gray clouds
We lose that island space of narrowing blue—
The man who hoards a casket, shuddering
Will press it closer to his aching heart,
If the deep reed bed should but tremble to
The wind that strays thro' its rustling depths, or
  wave
Its trembling shadows to the ambiguity
Of moonlight. So it fares with him who knows
The windings of the world and fain would cherish
All that he loves from its intrusion:
Distrust increases with increase of years,
She is the firstborn of Experience
And ye may know her by her stealthy shuffle
And the keen gray twinkle of her deep-sunk eye

6

And the rejectings of her anxious front
To gaze at her own shadow. If ye greet her,
Or pass your hand in hers, she will respond
With an uncordial and relaxing grasp,
As though she did repent her courtesy
E'en in the doing o't—but from her counsel
We learn that many a gay flower, which disperses
Incense to every wandering air, fades off
And grows to a poisonous berry, which gives death
To all who taste it—that the broider'd side
Of Life's fair tapestry, with its woven groups
Of gloomy imagery, and the inwrought splendour
Of flower and fruitage, sheweth fair to the eyes
Of inexperienced immaturity,
But unto those whose rarity of locks
The hand of Time hath salted, she exhibits
The dark reverse of it,
The intertwinings and rough wanderings
Of random threads and wayward colourings—
A mêlée and confusion of all hues,
Disorder of a system which seemed Order.
Yet never, in my gayest hour of Being,
Was I so sanguine as to deem my fate
Would with each longing of impatient Hope
Each gasp and indraw of the hasty breath
Sparkle like Oroonoko* in a tube,
Which even as it ignites and inflames
Doth change to bitter ashes.

* A name once given to the commonest sort of tobacco in
Virginia.—ED.

SCENE IV

Enter AMORET

MAGUS Here Amoret, a word with thee!

AMORET   Proceed.

MAGUS I am called hence by strong necessity.

AMORET Alas! and when shall Heaven's auspicious
    breath
    Restore thee to these longing eyes?

MAGUS   Perhaps
    E're yet again the silver moon shall fill
    The curvéd radiance of her glowing horns.

AMORET How in thy tedious absence shall I chide
    The lazy motion of the lagging hours?
    Hours will seem days.

MAGUS   Sweet Amoret I would
    Thy tongue were not at variance with thy heart.

AMORET True as the handle of the horologe,
    As ever moved by the works within,
    So move my lips responsive to my heart:
    True as the many-chorded Harp returns
    Harmonious answers to a master's touch—
    So speaks this tongue congenial to my Soul.

MAGUS It is not mine to draw aside the veil
    Of dark deception, or unmask the thoughts
    Of other minds—My Necromantic arts
    Could never teach me this—sooner might I
    Transmute this bodily form into some shape
    Of wingéd bird or lazy quadruped
    Or bloodless habitant of Ocean's wave.

AMORET Alas! and why should false suspicion's
    breath,
    With such ill-omened and pernicious words

8

Tarnish the lustre of my spotless fame?
MAGUS I cannot trace the windings of a heart,
The searchless windings of a woman's mind,
For that Egyptian labyrinth famed of old
With all its maze of avenues and chambers
Were nothing to it—like a lightsome feather
When put in balance with a ton of lead.
AMORET (*weeping*)
What weighty cause, what reason have I giv'n
That thou should'st treat me thus unkindly,
    Magus?
Have I not lent to thee my youth, my time,
And all that I possess? To thee o'er whom
Full eighty suns have roll'd, while these young eyes
Have barely seen a score, yet would I live
Embosom'd in the fulness of content,
Did not thy temper, fretful and morose,
Still find new themes to harp upon and rail,
Making the shadow of a sound reality,
And the thin air solidity of substance,
For thou art jealousy personified.
MAGUS Pass not too harsh a judgment on me, Amoret.
Causes however slight do oft give birth to
The same effects as spring from weightier reasons.
The little burning taper's tremulous ray
And th' inexhaustible fount of fire which lives
And emanates from the great Sun, would move
The Dial's circling shadows equally.
And, if thy nature in itself be fickle,
Remember that the windy vane will veer
To the Heaven's lightest murmuring, as well as
To the strong tempest's chidings; one light word,

One thoughtless look, may lead frail spirits as far
As the vice pre-meditated.
Who shall know man, or freely explicate
The many folds of character? or who
Shall bear the lamp of subtle scrutiny
Into the deep recesses of the heart?
Each Being is a world within himself,
A complicated Engine, whose main springs
Are circumstance and habit, and were this space
Of limited life a chain of centuries,
And each particular minute o't employ'd
In the developing another's nature,
'Twere all too short for th' purpose.
I have liv'd long and shall live longer, I
Have mix'd with life in all its variations,
I have visited the camp, the court, the mob,
The riotous tavern, the unruly Hell,
The penetrated hovel, the high palace,
I have had friends and they were stedfast, enemies
And they were bitter—I have wandered far
From th' utmost Arctic to its opposite,
I have seen the thievish Russ, the crusty Spaniard,
The bold, brave Switzer, the freehearted Scot,
The musical Italian, the proud Angle,
The volatile, light-heeled Frank, the sleepy Turk,
The money-loving and broad-bas'd Mynheer—
AMORET Illiberal innuendos and dark hints
Are gender'd of suspicion—she who views
All objects thro' a mighty magnifier
And multiplies to her diseased vision
Accumulation of anxieties.
MAGUS Well, Amoret, I will believe thee true

10

And faithful as the compass to the pole.
For in life's passage would I always look
Upon that side of things which sheweth fairest,
Else were our days but one continued gloom,
A weary scene of surmise and mistrust.
The breath of life blows chillingly enow
To nip our sweetest hopes, and heaven forefend
That we should waken bootless grievances—
When the keen Ether is condens'd with frost
Who would not cleave to th' sunny side o' th'
  wall?
And hark ye, Amoret, one word of counsel!
Close thou thy casement early, nor look down
At sound of querulous serenade or flute
Wooing the dewy wings o' th' midnight air
To carry upwards on their whispering down
Unto the gaping portals of thine ears
Its soothing luxury of tender tone—
Regard not thou the glancing of the eye—
The pressure of the hand—the easy lapse
Of honey'd words from amatory lips—
All this regard not—Now farewell; may Heaven
And the good Saints protect thee!

                                    [*Going*

AMORET   The like wish
Attend thee on thy way!
MAGUS (*returning*)   If I have said
Ought roughly or in anger—
AMORET   Think not of it!
Once more farewell—
MAGUS   Farewell, my own good Amoret,
And if my humour should sometimes show testy,

11

Impute it all unto the love I bear thee,
Which effervesceth of its own intensity,
And oftentimes mounts upward and boils over
Because of its own fervour.

[*Exit*

AMORET   Go thy ways!
Thou yellowest leaf on Autumn's wither'd tree!
Thou sickliest ear of all the sheaf! thou clod!
Thou fireless mixture of Earth's coldest clay!
Thou crazy dotard, crusted o'er with age
As thick as ice upon a standing pool!
Thou shrunken, sapless, wizen Grasshopper,
Consuming the green promise of my youth!
Go, get thee gone, and evil winds attend thee,
Thou antidote to love! thou bane of Hope,
Which like the float o' th' fisher's rod buoys up
The sinking line and by its fluctuations
Shows when the pang of Disappointment gnaws
Beneath it! But to me are both unknown:
I never more can hope and therefore never
Can suffer Disappointment.
He bears a charmed life and will outlast me
In mustiness of dry longevity,
Like some tough mummy wither'd, not decay'd—
His years are countless as the dusty race
That people an old Cheese and flourish only
In the unsoundest parts on't.
The big waves shatter thy frail skiff! the winds
Sing anything but lullabies unto thee!
The dark-hair'd Midnight grant no ray to thee,
But that of lightning, or the dreadful splendour
Of the conflicting wave! the red bolt scathe thee!

12

Why was I link'd with such a frowzy mate,
With such a fusty partner of my days?

Scene V   (*Enter* Devil)
    [Amoret *shrieks, covers her face with her hand and
        runs to the door.* Devil *brings her back and
        forces her into a chair*
Devil Madam! What's this? What? Railing? Fie!
    for shame!
    (Nay, sit you still and hear me.) Think you then
    To play Xantippe with impunity,
    Who gave her philosophical old spouse
    So choice and delicate a water bath
    To whet his appetite one frosty morning
    Before his breakfast? Do you hearken to me?
Amoret Ye saints defend me—I shall die with terror.
Devil. How, now, my dainty one, my delicate ward,
    My pretty piece of frail mortality,
    Where think you is the rendezvous of Saints,
    Where their celestial club-room, that you make
    A fretwork argent of your snowy fingers,
    And cast your jetty pupils up on high
    Until the blank, unanimated white
    Usurps the field of vision?
    A most unphilosophical conclusion!
    Point thy hands downward, turn thine eyes to the
        floor!
    There is a Heaven beneath this Earth as fair
    As that which roofs it here.
    Dost think that Heaven is local, and not rather
    The omnipresence of the glorified
    And liberated Spirit—the expansion

13

Of man's depress'd and fetter'd faculties
Into omniscience?

AMORET   O ye Powers have mercy!

DEVIL Have mercy, quoth'a! when had thy tongue
    mercy
Upon thy betters, mistress? Curb it straightly,
'Tis the most dangerous member of the Body—
Unto the wise a blessing and a benefit,
A healing balm of mild Persuasion,
A sewer up of rents, sweet Pity's oracle,
A curber of dissension's contumely—
But in the mouth of the improvident
Worse than an Adder's fang.
It prompts the brain to hatch, the hand to execute,
The heart to shake off conscience and the back
To throw away the burden of restraint,
The saucy foot to spurn Authority.
Faith and troth, Madam, if my fates had bid me
To tread the thorny path of life with thee,
If the indissoluble, firm-knit chain
Of fixed alliance in its sacred bond
Had joined the fortune of thy stars with mine,
Would I become a target of your taunts?
The mark and butt of your unruly tongue?
Would I be baffled, like the idle wave
Fuming and fretting on a changeless rock,
Without the power to make impression
On the obdurate nature of the stone?
Would I be hurried like the dust of the earth
With every gale of passion to and fro,
Or be the plaything of your haughtiness
To gibe and sneer at?

14

AMORET   Hence! Avaunt, foul fiend!
    Bear hence the terrors of thy crooked horns
    And the long windings of thy sinuous tail!
    Oh! that I could speak Latin, whose magic sounds
    And Elfin syllables might drive thee far
    To thy remotest Hell.
DEVIL   Ha! Ha! Ha! Ha!
    Now by my Devilship 'tis wondrous plain,
    Plain as the polish of a marble floor,
    Plain as the surface of a bowling green,
    Plain as the nose upon a Negro's face,
    That husbands are the veriest dolts in nature.
    Ye henpeck'd mates, who, like insensate drones,
    Doze out your sleepy melancholy days,
    Who twist and twine beneath th' oppression
    Of woman's will, did ever Nature leave
    To man on earth a want unsatisfied?
    Has she not planted in each towering hedge
    That fronts the King's highway, in each green
        wood
    That crowns the balmy summit of the hill
    A sovereign remedy to curb the power
    Of overbearing insolence and pride?
    Ye are all wrapt in apathy, else where
    Would ARGUMENTUM BACULINUM be?
    'Tis a most delicate physic, suited to
    All ages from the schoolboy to the wife.
    It quickens business, makes the lazy blood,
    Which heretofore was stagnant, circulate,
    'Tis the primeval origin of virtue,
    Moulding the mind to good, it checks the freaks
    Of growing vice i' th' heart; corrects the hardness

                        15

Of our ferocious natures like the iron
Which when most beaten is most ductile; thus
Men's natures are all malleable: should'st thou use
   them
Mildly, they turn again and trample thee;
But should'st thou hold and rein them straitly in,
And curb the mettled nature of their spirits,
When first they leave life's starting-post, they fear
   thee,
And fearing honour, honouring obey thee,
Obeying, love thee. Honour, love and fear
All meet in a bamboo. Oh! Heaven and Earth!
Why wilt thou crouch and bow and lick the dust
Whereon thy consort treads? Beat back the stream
And to the violence of the ridgéd waves
Oppose the massy stonework of thy power,
Though for awhile it roar and bound above
The opposition of thy barrier—
Yet raise thy dam up higher—higher still—
Till the submissive stream with silent course
Seek its far fount. She'll never rave again,
Unless in negligence or flexibility
Of yielding nature thou should'st leave some
   avenue
To her insinuating and sapping force,
(Which will not leave one stone unturn'd, until
She doth recover her dominion)
Some faithless fissure or uncemented hole,
Whence her ebullient spirit may leap forth,
At first in an attenuated stream,
Unto new contest, and enlarging straightly
May hurry thy frail mound down its rough bed,

16

And leave thee with one finger in thine eye
To wail the pliability which led thee
To trust thus far.

AMORET   I know not whence thou comest,
Nor who thou art, nor what thy message here,
Nor how I may exorcise thee, or drive
Thy troubled spirit to its biding-place.
If there be ought of pity in thy soul,
I do beseech thee leave me to my thoughts
And solitude.

DEVIL   Thoughts! Thoughts! what thoughts are thine
But evil and dishonour?

AMORET   Nay, I'll kneel
And pray thee to depart.

DEVIL   Out on thee, woman!
Devils are faithful to their trust.

AMORET   Alas!
Am I entrusted then to thee?

DEVIL   Dost weep?
Is that a tear which stains thy cheek? Nay—
now
It quivers at the tip-end of thy nose
Which makes it somewhat dubious from which
feature
It first had issue.

AMORET   I conjure thee—

DEVIL   Tears!
The rain of sentiment, the dews of feeling,
The beads of sensibility!
They are the coinage of a single wish.
I know that ye can summon them at will.

D   17

They are a woman's weapons, sword and shield,
Wherewith she braves remonstrance and breaks
    hearts—
Those faithful sluices never are drawn dry.
Even the withering heat of passion
But leads them forth in greater plenitude.
What! more! I know ye can command them,
    woman,
Even to the precise number, ten or twenty,
As suits occasion—
More yet? Methinks the cavity o' thy skull
Is brine i' th' room o' brains. More yet? at this
    rate
You'd float a ship o' the line.
This is the cogent stream wherewith ye turn
The mill-wheel of men's love (whose motion
Guides all the inner workings o' the heart)
And grind what grist ye please.

AMORET   I pray thee—
DEVIL Get thee to bed—yet stay—but one word
    more—
Let there be no somnambulations,
No colloquy of soft-tongued whisperings
Like the low hum of the delighted bee
I' th' calyx of a lily—no kerchief-waving!
No footfalls i' th' still night! Lie quietly,
Without the movement of one naughty muscle,
Still as a kernel in its stone, and lifeless
As the dull yoke within its parent shell,
Ere yet the *punctum saliens* vivify it.
I know ye are perverse, and ever wish,
Maugre my wholesome admonitions,

18

To run obliquely like the bishop at chess,
But I'll cry "check" to ye, I warrant ye
I'll prove a "stalemate" to ye.

AMORET (*half aside*)

In all conscience
My mate is stale enough.

DEVIL   Do'st mutter? how?
Would you outface the devil, Insolence?
Or tweak me like St. Dunstan by the nose,
Who scarified my smeller for a twelvemonth?
Who would cast seeds i' th' ocean? who would graft
Good counsel's fruits upon a stock so sterile?
Oh! Amoret! there is no honour in thee;
Thou art the painted vision of a dream,
Whose colours fade to nothing, a fair rainbow
Mocking the tantalized sight, an airy bubble,
O'er whose bright surface fly the hues of light,
As if to hide the nothingness within.
Few will bear sounding—cast the plummet in
And it will draw up mud, vile, worthless mud.
Gaze on the mirror of the silver lake
In its clear picture deftly pencilling
The soft inversion of the tremulous woods,
But probe it not to th' bottom—weeds, rank weeds,
Darkness and swarming reptiles harbour there.
Now go and ponder on my words. Begone.
                         [*Exit* AMORET

I am in troth a moralising devil,
Quite out o' my element; my element, fire.
Then come my spirit, with thy torch light up
The strongest flame of thine ability,

19

Use all thine efforts—work thy passage, as
The restless rushing of a fiery flood
Within the hollow and sonorous earth.
Now to my charge—I must be violent, fierce,
And put that ugly disposition on
Which is my portion by inheritance
From my great grandsire Lucifer—Good lack!
I'll make the scurvy-pated villains skip
As they were mad, e'en though they thronged about
    me,
As thick as Beelzebub on Beelzebub,
Alias as thick as horseflies on horse-dung.
'Twill be a troublesome office. Nay, by Phlegethon,
I'd rather be the chilly watch, whose voice
Sounds midnight through the length o' the hazy
    streets
In some great city, by the misty light
O' th' fumigated moon, than guard a woman.
When will the reign of feminine intrigues
Of female politics and folly cease?
It will be much about that time, methinks,
When this dark field of earth shall be sow'd
    thick
With the gay stars of Heav'n and the keen plough-
    share
Shall trench deep furrows in the inverted sky;
When his triple mitred Holiness shall become
An arrant Protestant, and all their Eminences
Shall be *unboiled* into th' humility
Of black canonicals; when a second Becket
Shall thunder excommunication
From out his lordly see of Canterbury;

When Summer shall be Winter, and Spring
   Autumn;
When cold shall rarify and heat condense;
When Almacks shall become the rendezvous
Of burly citizens and citizens' wives,
And Lady J—y wearied shall throw down
The reins of Fashion and—think better things;
When high soul'd man shall walk upon his head,
Whcn Colonel B—y shall shake hands with De-
   cency
And read or write a sermon.
So! So! methinks in good truth I have hemm'd in
My proposition with a sweeping circle
Of insurmountable improbabilities.
Yon taper sinks i' th' socket; Time wears quickly,
Yet treads in shoes of felt. What is't o'clock?
                         [Going to the timepiece
Half after midnight! These mute moralizers,
Pointing to the unheeded lapse of hours,
Become a tacit eloquent reproach
Unto the dissipation of this Earth.
There is a clock in Pandemonium,
Hard by the burning throne of my Great Grand-
   sire,
The slow vibrations of whose pendulum,
With click-clack alternation to and fro,
Sound "EVER, NEVER!" thro' the courts of Hell,
Piercing the wrung ears of the damn'd that writhe
Upon their beds of flame, and, whensoe'er
There may be short cessation of their wailings,
Through all the boundless depth of fires is heard
The shrill and solemn warning "EVER, NEVER."

Then bitterly, I trow, they turn and toss
And shriek and shout, to drown the thrilling
    note—
                    [Looking again at the timepiece
Half after midnight! Wherefore stand I here?
Methinks my tongue runs twenty knots an hour:
I must unto mine office.
                           [Exit abruptly

ACT II

SCENE I [MAGUS'S *cottage with the wood and lake*
in the distance. Enter DEVIL *and takes his*
station before the cottage door attired in a cap
and gown.

DEVIL The starry fires of yon Chrystalline vault
Are waning, and the airy-footed Night
Will soon withdraw the dismal solitude
Of her capacious pall, wherewith she clouds
Yon mighty and illimitable sky,
Placing a death-like colour in all things,
Monopolizing all the varied Earth
With her dim mantle—

[*A pause*

Oh! ye eyes of Heaven,
Ye glorious inextinguishable lights,
High blazing mid the lone solemnity
Of night and silence, shall the poor worm, Man,
The creature of this solitary earth,
Presume to think his destiny enroll'd
In your almighty everlasting fires?
Shall this poor thing of melancholy clay,
This lone ephemeris of one small hour,
Proudly suppose his little fate incribed
In the magnificent stars? What have the worlds
Of yon o'er arching Heav'n—the ample spheres
Of never-ending space, to do with Man?
And some romantick visionaries have deem'd
This petty clod the centre of all worlds.
Nay—even the Sun himself, the gorgeous Sun,

23

Pays homage to it. Ha! Ha! Ha! Poor Man,
Thou summer midge!—Oh, ye shine bravely now
Through the deep purple of the summer sky,
I know that ye are Earths as fair and fairer
And mightier than this I tread upon—
For I have scaled your mountains, to whose cones
Of most insuperable altitude
This Earth's most glorious Eminences and heights
All pil'd and heap'd upon each other's brows,
And massed and kneaded to one common sub-
   stance,
Were but a molehill.
And I have swum your boundless seas, whose
   waves
Were each an ocean of this little orb,
Yet know I not your natures, or if that
Which we call palpable and visible
Is condensation of firm particles.
O suns and spheres and stars and belts and
   systems,
Are ye or are ye not?
Are ye realities or semblances
Of that which men call real?
Are ye true substance? are ye anything
Except delusive shows and physical points
Endow'd with some repulsive potency?
Could the Omnipotent fill all space, if ye
Or the least atom in ye or the least
Division of that atom (if least can dwell
In infinite divisibility) should be impenetrable?
I have some doubt if ye exist when none
Are by to view ye; if your Being alone

Be in the mind and the intelligence
Of the created? should some great decree
Annihilate the sentient principle
Would ye or would ye not be non-existent?
'Tis a shrewd doubt—

　　　　　　　　　　[*A sound of footsteps heard*
　　　　　　　　　But softly! who comes here?
What stealthy foot invades these secret woods?
Tis some Alcinoüs or Eurymedon
Who haunts this wild and wanton Amoret!
Perchance some smooth-chinn'd Tyro just emerg-
　　　ing
From Hobbledehoyhood's twilight, and elated
With the dark sproutings of incipient beard,
Or some sleek monk enveloping the bronze
Of his dark cheek beneath his rusty cowl.
Now will I cloak myself, and thus conceal
This grim, fantastic nose and these wide lips,
That staring shew the black and knotty teeth
That fence my jaws like hedge-stakes (I have lost
Much of original beauty since my fall),
Now will I smooth the harshness of my voice
Into a feminine croak, tuck up my tail,
And thus unsex myself.

　　　　　　　　　　[*Draws the hood over his face*

SCENE II *Enter* ANTONIO

ANTONIO Ye gracious Heav'ns
Is't Amoret, the rosebud of whose cheeks
Is preferable to a suit at Law
Successfully unravell'd—the rich sound
Of whose harmonious and most silver voice
Steals sweeter on mine ear than does the chink
Of golden or of silver boys* wrung out
From the hard client's gripe—whose delicate smile
Is worth a ten day's fee? So! here I come
To pay my devoirs at the shrine of beauty.
For this, as soon as e'er the deep-mouth'd voice
Of the most lonely tempest ceas'd to shake
Heaven's pillars of the solid earth, I paced
This wild and marshy wood; for this have burrs
Clung to me as thou seest, more in number
Than cases in the Court of Common Pleas;
For this the drizzly trees and dripping shrubs
Shower'd on me as I hurried past, more thickly
Than diamonds on a birthnight.
DEVIL (*speaking in an undertone*)   Gentle Sir,
You overrate yourself. True love had scorn'd
The petty hindrances of wind and weather—
Gods! why a lover is all heat and fire,
A mustard pot, a very pepper-box,
And his internal warmth of temperament
Might guard him from external cold—Ay! though
Thou had'st bolted thro' the very teeth o' the
storm
Bareheaded, every gusty drop of Heav'n

* "Yellow Boys"—early slang for guineas.—ED.

Had run off hissing from thy glowing surface,
As from a bar of red hot iron. Believe me,
If thou wert a true lover, wind and rain
Would have no power on thee. 'Twas never known
That one who lov'd most ardently and truly
Was ever laid up for a single se'nnight
With a red nose.

ANTONIO   Now on mine honour—
DEVIL   Prithee,
If thou desirest ought of credit with me,
Most commendable and good Antonio,
Swear not upon thine honour! It is rare
With those of thy most honourable cut,
As is the desert fire-born biped sprung
From its own ashes. If thou swearest, swear
By that thou lovest best.

ANTONIO   Then by my fees—
DEVIL Ay—there the right nail's struck upon the head.
ANTONIO Or by thy dearer self—
DEVIL   Now, prithee, lie not,
Keep thy first oath—thy fees are dearer to thee.

ANTONIO Well, by my fees (that I may honour thee
And put an end to dissertation)
I know a most true lover Leontio,
That hath a nose as red as a skinned eel
Or pickled cabbage steeped in vinegar,
And flaming as a scarlet mailed lobster,
Although he hath a lady in his head.

DEVIL Then it proceedeth from the warmth within,
Not from the cold without.

ANTONIO   How prove you that,
Fair Amoret? the case is clearly mine,

27

Let A be then the heart and B the nose,
True love is centre'd in the heart. What then?
It follows that the heat's in A the heart
And not in B the nose—PROBATUM EST.
D E V I L Good Sir, the case is this—the lover's heart
Is so o'ercharged with the secret flames
That do consume its melancholy core,
That all the superfluity of love,
And the redundant heat, escaping thence,
Take up their station in the lover's nose
Which thence doth show like beetroot.
A N T O N I O   SATIS EST;
A truce to dissertation. Let us use
More soft discussion, gentle paramour.
Gaze all around thee—see yon canopy
Of the eternal boundless Heavens—yon host
Of all the congregated stars—this earth,
This fair green plain of the luxuriant earth—
Breathe, fair one, breathe the soul inspiring air
Full of the all-heavenly incense wafted from
The groves, the fruits, the gaily-blooming flowers,
Which the rough tempest hath but wak'd to beauty
More fresh than heretofore. Is this a time
For disputation? Starlight, incense, flowers,
And two young loving hearts!
D E V I L   Talk not of love,
Thou need'st must wait cessation of the storm—
A N T O N I O What, harping on th'old string again?
D E V I L   Ay, Sirrah,
Did not Leander swim the roaring main,
The boundless Hellespont (as Homer calls it)
On such a dark and dismal night as this was

Half one good hour ago?

ANTONIO   And perish'd too.

DEVIL Go to—thou art no lover!

ANTONIO   Thou beliest me—
I am an honest, true and proper lover,
A gentle, comely, comfortable lover,
A well-proportion'd and most gracious lover,
As ever woman set her eyes upon.

DEVIL Thou knowest that my spouse did journey
        hence
At midnight, yet dids't thou delay thy coming
Until the storm had swept above thine head.

ANTONIO Inimitable mistress of my heart,
I sate in judgment on my love and judged it,
I issued out a WRIT against my conscience,
And sent a MITTIMUS unto my soul,
I tried and prov'd it thoroughly and found
That it was free from blame—PROBATUM EST.
But come, unveil those eyes, whose dazzlingness
Shoots forth more deadly and more certain shafts
Than those the curly-headed Indian sends
By force of breath from out the echoing tube.

DEVIL 'Tis a chill night—I fear the damp—I cannot
Uncloak myself in such wise.

ANTONIO   Will it please you
To enter in?

DEVIL   Proceed! I follow thee.

ANTONIO Thy deeds do give the lie unto thy tongue,
Thou art as motionless as Lot's wife.

DEVIL   Begone,
On pain of my displeasure—hie thee hence—
I will attend thee in as many moments

As there are peas in a pod or teats upon
The gentle cow's most elegant dugs, or on
Old ALMA MATER,* which are two or three—
Albeit she hath the credit for some dozens.
[*Exit* A N T O N I O *into the Cottage.* D E V I L *throws
up his hood and proceeds*

SCENE III.

DEVIL Now, most sweet Sir, I have thee,
Thou shalt repent of thine audacity
Wherewith upheld, thus buoyantly and highly,
Thou spurrest thy desire to lawless deeds
Of bronze-brow'd arrogance, and darest thus
To climb into the solitary fold
Of thy good neighbour, and to cull the fleece
Which he esteemeth best—but I will prove
No tame, submissive, crouching centinel:
But I will take such fearful hold on thee,
As doth the wayward irritable crab
On the poor traveller—thou art thoughtless, young,
Full of high mettled hopes, hot blooded, sanguine,
With haughty self-sufficiency of nature,
Which is the attribute of thy green years
That brook not sober meditation.
Visions of happiness do float before thee,
Gay-gilded figures and most eloquent shapes,
Moulded by Fancy's gentle fingering
To the appearance of reality,
With youthful expectations and fond dreams,

* The Goddess Rhea or Cybele, wife of Saturn and mother
of the Gods, often represented with a number of breasts as
an emblem of fertility.—ED.

All rendered sunlike by the light of youth,
Which glances on them, flit before thine eyes:
But these shall be pinch'd out of thee ere morn—
There shall be no sound place within thy person;
Thou shalt be all the colours of the rainbow,
With bruises, pinches, weals, ET COETERA;
And various as the motley colour'd slime,
Which floats upon the standing pool, wherein
Do breed all kinds of reptiles—creeping things,
Vile jellies and white spawn and loathsome newts.
But come descend, thou penthouse:

                        [Draws down his hood
                          Hither comes

One Pharmaceutus an apothecary,
A mad, drug-dealing, vile apothecary—
A thing of gallipots and boluses,
Lean, lanthorn-jaw'd, splay handed, pasty fac'd,
Hard favour'd and loose-jointed, ill proportion'd,
Whose hips do roll on castors, and whose love
Is nauseous as his physic—Faugh! I know not
How I can keep my character. But here
He comes and brings his fetid atmosphere
About his person.

SCENE IV   *Enter* PHARMACEUTUS.

                 Welcome, gentle Sir.
PHARMACEUTUS Welcome, fair lady, may the bloom
    of joy
And the medicinal virtue of all health
Spread the fair carpet of thy roseate face
With its gay colouring.

DEVIL (*aside*).   How cursedly
    He stinks of assafœtida. Art cold?
    Dost shake and shiver?
PHARMACEUTUS   Marry do I.
DEVIL   What?
    Did'st not escape the tempest?
PHARMACEUTUS   No, i' faith,
    I am half palsied with frigidity,
    I'm below zero, I am perfect ice
    Congeal'd to all intents and purposes,
    My nose, my ears, and each particular toe,
    Will quit their station—hark! my grinders chatter
    Like castanets, or fulling mills. Let's in—
    And hark ye, some of Magus's brown stout;
    I'll smoke a pipe of comfortable shag-tail
    By the fireside with thee. Wilt let us in?
DEVIL Ay, presently.
PHARMACEUTUS   'Sdeath, Madam, instantly!
    Or thaw me with a look, a loving look
    From the full lustre of thy melting eyes!
    'Sblood! thou art hooded and pent up as tightly
    As a sea-urchin.
DEVIL   Is't not fitting, prithee?
    Did'st thou not talk of nose dropping?
PHARMACEUTUS   Ay, Madam,
    The storm hath left a chill i' the air, 'tis damp,
    Rheumatic mists are whitening in the marshes,
    And pale-fac'd Ague wanders all abroad.
    But let us enter; eh?
    [*Here* ANTONIO *half opens the cottage door and
        exclaims*
ANTONIO   Where art thou, fair one?
                          32

DEVIL Here, sirrah, with this gentleman!

ANTONIO (*coming forward*)   How now!
   What! with this scurvy rascal, this poor drug,
   This compound of all ugliness, this dog,
   This Ipecacuanha, this emetic,
   This wall-eyed monster, this anomaly,
   This piece of speckled parchment, this vile patch-
      work,
   Whose sallow and carbuncled face resembles
   A red design upon a yellow ground?

PHARMACEUTUS Pills! plasters! powders! poul-
   tices! what now!

ANTONIO Sirrah! I'll knock thy grinders down thy
   throat.

PHARMACEUTUS (*staggering backwards*)
   Bole*! Borax! Blister! Balsam! Bark! What now?

ANTONIO Thou hocus-pocus of deformity!
   Thou scum! thou outcast of society!

PHARMACEUTUS Galls! Garlick! ginger! guiacum!
   what now?

ANTONIO I'll punch thee into jelly—scatter thee
   To the four Winds of Heav'n—thou scarcerow,
      thou!

DEVIL Good words—sweet words, Antonio, prithee.

PHARMACEUTUS   Bless thee,
   My honey of squills, my oil of almonds, bless thee!
   Thou hast a good heart.

ANTONIO   How! you sorry rascal!
   Do you make love to the lady?

PHARMACEUTUS   Mercy on us!

---

* "Bole armeniac"—an astringent earth brought from
Armenia and used as an astringent and styptic.—ED.

The man is mad—he must be blooded.

ANTONIO   How

Do'st prate, thou vile anatomy? Bind up
Thy jaws or by the Devil and his dam
I'll make a gap within thy villainous throat
And pour libations of thy wretched blood
Unto this Goddess. What! thou fulsome scrag!
Woulds't thou make love with that untoward chin
Hook'd and turn'd upwards like a Chinese shoe?

PHARMACEUTUS Beshrew my heart but thou art wondrous mad,
Mad as a March hare, and as hot as Cowhage*
Without molasses.

ANTONIO   Hang dog!

DEVIL   Peace, Antonio!

Why, thou art 80, man, by Reaumur's scale,
And more than twice as much by Fahrenheit,
And the unconquerable turbulence
And violent usage of your fiery temper,
Expanded by the heat of passion,
Will burst the tube of temperance. Methinks
I am afraid to look upon you, lest
Your head should part in twain, and thence should issue
The subtle fluid which distends you so.

ANTONIO Thou fairest excellence of what is most
Excelling in all nature! loveliest mixture
Of all that is most lovely! is it tolerable
That this sad miscreant, this uncouth Behemoth,

* "Cowhage"—a tropical plant *Mucuna pruriens*, with stinging hairs on its pods, used medicinally.—ED.

Thus monstrous in his vanity of mind,
And loathsome in deformity of person,
Each, render'd still more horrible by each,
When thus contrasted—is it tolerable
That he should raise the base and abject scum
Of his vile thoughts so high, and thus presume
To come within the rich and glorious sphere
Of thine attractions? Fie! it must not be.

DEVIL Did I not say that thou wert hotly rais'd
By thine inexorable fire of anger
As high as "WATER-BOIL"?

ANTONIO   No—by the Law!
It is but " SUMMER-HEAT."

DEVIL   I prithee cloak not
Thy faults beneath the colouring of fair names,
Nor modify the wild unevenness
Of thy capricious disposition
With sounds of softest import: for i'faith
Thy Spirits boil at least!

ANTONIO   That fusty wretch
Hath roused them up to fermentation.

PHARMACEUTUS   Sir,
You are as bitter as Alum.

ANTONIO   You, as foul
As your own fœtid pills.

PHARMACEUTUS   And you as brisk
As bottled beer.

ANTONIO   Do you chop logic with me
You dunderhead?

PHARMACEUTUS   Who? I, Sir? No, Sir.

ANTONIO   Sirrah!
If thou presumest to give thy fool's tongue

35

The damning license of a repartee,
I'll have the substance of thy cursed brains
Pounded and beat up in a red-hot mortar
And with a burning pestle; of thine hide
Will I make ass-skin breeches.

PHARMACEUTUS   Mercy on us!
The man is hypochondriack or hysterical—
Here! here! bring spirits of hartshorn and burnt
    feathers
And clap hot bricks to 's feet!

ANTONIO   I'll knit thee up,
And thou shalt hang in the mid-air as prettily
As a vile cur that sucks hen's eggs, while I
Will sing thy parting elegy, and thou
Shalt beat the due observance of the time
With thy unwieldy toes! Thou shalt be balanc'd
As neatly as a difficult case between
Two able pleaders!

DEVIL   Fie, Antonio, fie!
Excess of violence becomes thee not,
It sits as ill upon thy shoulders as
Love on an old maid with a hump-back.

ANTONIO   Or
On this same Pharmaceutus. Ha! ha! ha!

PHARMACEUTUS Now by Hippocrates, by Galen,
    Celsus
And the great Boerhaave—the dazzling sun
And star of Medical science—I do think
Thy wits are on the turn. Let's feel thy pulse,
Is't feverish or low? Give me a fleshbrush
That I may rub thee into sense—

ANTONIO   How now!

36

Thou most illiterate whelp, thou bristly cub,
Whom thy great Mother Bear hath never lick'd
To ought that may be called proportion!
Why! thou dead idiot, woulds't thou thus behave
As I were mad? in troth and faith I were so
If I should bear with thee. I should deserve
Commission of lunacy preferr'd against me
By the Lord Mayor.

PHARMACEUTUS   Fair Sir, I do presume
That you have heard the useful apothegm
That "Anger is short madness."

ANTONIO   Villainous wretch—

PHARMACEUTUS Here! pills of aloes! rhubarb!
spanish soap!

ANTONIO Woulds't thou not madden ought beneath
the sun
With thine accursed clucking?

PHARMACEUTUS   Gentle Sir,
Be not enraged—the stormy voice of wrath,
The lifting of the hand, the clenched fist,
And the wild glare of the tumultuous eye,
The broken interrupted words, which sound
Hollowly, like a bruis'd tin-kettle

ANTONIO   Oaf!

PHARMACEUTUS Th' inflation of the fiery cheeks,
blown up
With wind of idle passion, whence proceeds
The flushing of the face like the red clouds
Upon a blowy morning—

ANTONIO   Loon!

DEVIL   Be still,
Antonio, let us hear him out.

37

PHARMACEUTUS   All these
        Betoken anger which is madness. These
        Disorder all the animal functions, these
        Puzzle the progress of the chyle* and hurt
        The process of digestion.
ANTONIO   Curses on thee!
        When the next sessions sit, i' faith I'll have thee
        Indicted for a publick nuisance to
        His Majesty's loving subjects.
PHARMACEUTUS   Now, by Galen,
        Thou art as fine a subject for Phlebotomy
        As ever came to my inspection.
        I prithee let me breathe a vein, 'twill do thee
        An ample service.
                [*Here* A N T O N I O *raises his fist to strike him*
                    No—no—not the hand!
        I never bleed there, look ye, here's my instrument,
        The neck, the nape o' th' neck, Sir!
ANTONIO   The grim'd Imps
        Of Hell arrest thee at the Devil's suit!
        The red fiend ride thee into Chancery,
        Which is the worst curse I can vent upon thee!
DEVIL A most ungentlemanly wish, Antonio,
        Deserving objurgation—A propos,
        The Devil is an ill thing to be jested with;
        What if he should be standing by thee now,
        Speaking as I do—dress'd as I am? What
        If HIS TENEBRIOUS BITUMENSHIP
        Should be in hearing o' thee?
ANTONIO   Why, my Amoret,
        Thou art an angel and he dare not venture—

            * "Chyle"—intestinal fluid.—ED.

                    38

DEVIL   A fallen one, I grant ye.
ANTONIO   If a fallen one,
     So many sparks of thine ethereal nature
     Yet linger round thee as to make thy presence
     A portion of the Heaven thou hast fallen from.
DEVIL   Older and wiser, my good counsellor,
     An hour may change thy humour.
ANTONIO   Ay, the section
     Of one small minute (if 'twere spent with thee)
     Nay, the minutest point of time in which
     The inconceivable velocity
     Of light can travel thro' one barley-corn
     Of the blue Ether, were enough to raise me
     (Providing always it were spent with thee)
     From out my present humour, which is that
     Of the strong sea when in its ridg'd advance
     Bruised by the inroad of a vassal river,
     Or an enchaféd plaintiff face to face
     With the defendant.
DEVIL   In the mind of youth
     And pertinacious inexperience
     A hasty judgment sheweth like green fruit!
     The more unripe and immature it be,
     The harder clings it to its parent bough.
ANTONIO   Thou art the first o' thy sex that e'er found
        fault with
     The judgment   of   that   man   who   call'd   thee
        "Angel."
     I am immutable in nothing, save
     The love I bear thee—but behold who is't
     Comes swaggering hither? Why, what wants he
        here?

39

Methinks he seems a sailor by his swing;
His hat is cocked obliquely on his brow,
One eye is null and void or shut in waggery,
The never failing tokens of a rascal—
His arms are fix'd a kimbo, his left cheek
Protruded by a quid—what varlet's this?
Why wends he hither?

SCENE VI   *Enter* STEPHANIO.

STEPHANIO Blood and thunder, messmates,
     It seems I've run aground here.
ANTONIO   True!
PHARMACEUTUS   Ay, true!
ANTONIO How! dost thou stand in bodily fear of us?
STEPHANIO No, by the Devil and his dam!
DEVIL (*aside*)   That's I
     And mother Hecate.
ANTONIO   How is then thy case
     So ruinous and unwholesome?
STEPHANIO   Split my timbers!
     Thou art a lawyer and thus ruinous,
     And thou a nauseous apothecary,
     And thus unwholesome. Why! we sailors call
     Our sharks, sea-lawyers, and our lump fish, doctors.
     Have I run foul of ye? how got ye first
     Ahead o' me? Why! I came cutting hither
     With a fresh breeze i' my stern.
ANTONIO   With what intent?
STEPHANIO Bound from the cape of hope to th' port
     of love,
     To win the prize in yon rich galleon there.

40

ANTONIO What! can the heavenly essence of high love
       And all the little tendernesses, which
       Make up the catalogue of love, inhabit
       Such tenement as that thy breast affords?
       Why, art thou bona fide then in love?
STEPHANIO I tell thee, fellow, I'm half drown'd in
       love.
ANTONIO I'faith! I see that thou art half seas over.
STEPHANIO How! you landlubber, do you banter
       me?
       My senses are all founder'd in deep love,
       My cables rotted and my timbers beaten
       In by the force of love!
ANTONIO   And wilt thou place
       Thy claim in opposition to mine?
       Oyer and terminer! what misdemeanour
       Wilt thou be guilty of?
STEPHANIO   And who art thou?
       Thou cock-boat—thou poor cock-boat—thou mere
       shallop
       Varnished and painted, whose weak delicate planks
       Would shrink beneath a cap full o' wind!
PHARMACEUTUS   But I—
STEPHANIO And thou, sad, leaky, crack'd and bulg-
       ing hull,
       Wilt thou too tow thy sluggishness within
       Reach of my bomb-shot?
ANTONIO   Marry! here come more
       To stretch the thread of my poor Patience
       Into so thin and spidery a fibre
       That it will crack, unless the vexing grasp
       Of these uncomely interruptions

Relax the hold they've ta'en on't—
What man of points is this who cometh first,
In whose whole stature is no wavy line,
No flexure but what is abrupt and sudden?
His eyebrows have no arch, his hair is gather'd
Conewise upon his squar'd and narrow brow,
His thin dry lips seem parallel straight lines,
His red and angular and shapeless nose
Shows like a Gyron* gules in Heraldry,
And his sharp chin so narrow'd to a point,
That if 'twere possible his neck could bend
'Twould perforate and pierce his collar bone.

SCENE VII *Enter* ANGULO, CAMPANO, BENE-
DICT

ANGULO Most glorious luminary, round whose light,
Attracted by thy Majesty of Grace
We make our lowly revolutions,
Exert not thy centrifugal force upon me
But gently lead me to thee, by the power
Of thy centripetal might, that so I may
By due progression fall within thine arms!
CAMPANO 'Faith, 'tis a garrison well 'curtainéd'!
And it hath much of 'crown-work'!
STEPHANIO   So say I.
Ho! Madam, lower your colours!
ANGULO   Prithee, heed us
Nor shroud thyself in envious eclipse!

* "Gyron"—an "ordinary" of triangular shape used in
Heraldry.—ED.

42

Thou seest we encompass thee like satellites!
DEVIL Right, Angulo! and, sooth, it gratifies
My woman's vanity to see ye stand thus,
Myself the centre of the circle which
My charms have bow'd unto my vassalage!
But there be those among you upon whom
My looks fall distantly, and those on whom
The soft expression of mine eyes emits
A nearer and more partial ray.
ANGULO   Nay, pardon me—
The radii of a circle are all equal
Unto each other, my good Amoret,
The centre of it equally remov'd
From any point in the periphery.
BENEDICT Take heed not of the ungodly! I do
     come
To give thee ghostly consolation,
But find thee thus encircled with a crew
Of most ungracious sinners, led astray
By machinations of the evil one.
DEVIL (*aside*) True to a hair!
BENEDICT   Now, by our blessed Lady,
Hearken not to these fleshly minded men,
Vessels of wrath, the stumbling-blocks of life,
(Whom God requite hereafter for their deeds!)
But let us go and count our beads together.
I have a piece of the true cross, inclosed
In chrystal, which I'll show thee.
                    [*Pulling* DEVIL *after him*
STEPHANIO   Avast! avast! hi!
Get under weigh, my lads! what all at anchor?
Yare! yare! you see he's towing her away.

43

CAMPANO (*to* BENEDICT)

 And so you think to carry it by sap;
 We'll countermine you though. Halt, holy rascal!

BENEDICT Ave Maria! what a speech was that!

 Off, sinner! look ye! here's the blessed Virgin!

 [*Shewing her image*

 Woulds't thou impede the saving of a soul?

ANTONIO Why, who art thou, who with thy raiséd
 forehead,

 Curl'd lip, and archéd brow, woulds't beat us back,
 Squinting thro' thy green leeky eyes, and shaking
 Thy carroty locks, thus smoothly combed upon
 Thine austere front—who treadest on this earth
 As though thou wert not of it? who art thou?

BENEDICT One that would hold no converse with
 thee. Off!

 My soul rejects thee, sinner, and my hair
 Doth bristle at thy gross impiety, like
 Some baited Boar when blown on by the breathings
 Of the rude dog.

ANTONIO Thou hog in a high wind!
 Thou barrel-bellied sanctity!

BENEDICT Avaunt!
 You excommunicated heretic!

ANTONIO Oh! you tithe pig, and you would worm
 your way

 With that demurity of countenance,
 That frozen simulation of innocence
 Into your neighbour's strongholds?

CAMPANO Not so fast, sir,
 We'll stick a *cheval de frise* within the breach
 And beat him backward.

44

BENEDICT *(crossing himself)*

Ave Maria! what a speech was that!
Off, sinner! look ye, here's the blessed Virgin *(shewing her*
Would'st thou impede the saving of a soul? *image)*

ANTONIO

Why who art thou, who with thy raised front forehead
Curl'd lip & arched brow would'st beat us back
Squinting thro' thy green-leeky eyes & shaking
Thy carroty locks, that smoothly comb'd upon
Thine austere front — who treadest on this earth
As though thou wert not of it? Who art thou?

BENEDICT

One that would hold no converse with thee. Off!

CAMPANO

Hear, hear! he braves us.

STEPHANIO

Board ~~Slay~~ him.

ANGULO

Warring planets!
Here's bullying Mars *(TO STEPHANIO)* & Mercury, prince of thieves
And this old crafty Saturn *(to Benedict)* all at variance *(To Antonio)*
For Venus!

DEVIL

                    Gentlemen, this is not fitting
That ye with noisy & contentious brawls
And dissonance of ~~voices~~ tongues ~~should~~ thus disturb
The sober, drowsy, stealthy-footed night.
And rudely wake her echoes, shaking thus
These peaceful dew-drops from the boughs above us
Rather come in & if ye be inclin'd
To exalt your voices send them forth in songs
Glees, catches, merry madrigals, & such like

ANGULO   Warring planets!
    Here's bullying MARS with front as red as fire.
    Here's Mercury and he's the hottest o' ye
    And also as they say, the prince of thieves
    With this old crafty Saturn who exceedeth
    The rest in bulk, and all at variance
    For Venus—why, who'll square the difference?
STEPHANIO The ship yaws.
DEVIL   Gentlemen, this is not fitting
    That ye with noisy and contentious brawls
    And dissonance of tongues should thus disturb
    The sober, drowsy, stealthy-footed night,
    And rudely wake her echoes, shaking thus
    These peaceful dewdrops from the boughs above
      us.
    Rather come in and, if ye be inclin'd
    To exalt your voices, send them forth in songs,
    Glees, catches, merry madrigals, and such like
    'Till the roof totter o'er ye!
BENEDICT   Be it so.
    'Tis good to be afflicted. I will enter.
ANTONIO The Devil take the hindmost!
DEVIL   Well said, lawyer!
        [*Exeunt into the Cottage. Manet* DEVIL

45

Scene VIII.

DEVIL   O Race of Vipers, what should hinder me
        From crushing ye to nothing? O vile wasps,
        That flying round the honey'd vase dispute
        Who first shall dare immersion, could I take ye
        And dashing ye upon the earth could bruise
        Each impotent passion out o' ye, 'twere well;
        But if I left one spark of life in ye,
        The slightest glimmerings of existence, straightly
        Your teeming and prolific brains would hatch
        Conceptions of new vice, and, by and by,
        When the strong hand of chastisement relax'd,
        Ye would run down the steep ascent again
        Into the sink from whence ye were exalted,
        And would return to the forbidden thing
        With renovated zest. In after life
        Were punishment the herald of reform
        Th' infliction o't were good: but who shall fashion
        Clay that is hard and untenacious?
        Reform is rarer seen in after-life
        Than a rose i' th' brows of winter. Hark! I hear ye
        Head over ears in controversy and strife,
        I must unto ye and at any rate
        I'll thwart your present schemings—
        Bluebeard and Hickathrift! but I'll kick up
        The Devil of a Row, or more correctly
        The Row of a Devil.
        Belial, Abaddon, Astaroth, Asmodeus,
        Turn up your smoky eyes, ingrained with soot,
        And envy me the pranks which I shall play.
        Said I, Asmodeus? 'faith, he was a craven and a
           ninny and scar'd with the fume of fish-liver,

46

which I do much marvel, whether it were own'd by Pike, Turbot, Salmon, or Sturgeon—or what fish liver ever possessed such puissant and devil-driving abilities. But, by Styx, they may broil half the fry that swims, before my Devilship would budge an inch.

[Exit into the Cottage

ACT III

SCENE I (*A room in the cottage, a table laid out with meats, wines, etc.* DEVIL, ANTONIO, PHARMACEUTUS, STEPHANIO, ANGULO, CAMPANO *and* BENEDICT *at table.*)

DEVIL Here! push the bottle to Antonio,
    He's a choice spirit, whose wit shows brightest when
    Burnish'd by wine. Drink sippingly, but not
    So as to surfeit th' senses; only kindle
    The combination of images
    From whose collision leaps the brilliant spark
    Of Heaven-born wit.

ANTONIO   Fair Amoret, I drink
    Unto the absence of thy loving husband.

                      [*To* STEPHANIO
    Hark ye, Stephanio, ply the Monk with wine,
    Mellow his austere nature.

STEPHANIO   Mr. Benedict
    The bottle is with you.

BENEDICT   With me! O Shame!
    Take it away! it doth pollute mine eye-sight.
    The simple mountain stream that gusheth down
    The cavern doth suffice my natural wants
    And the few roots that spring uncultivated.

ANTONIO Tush! man, thy fair round juicy corporation
    Doth give the lie unto thine utterance!

48

An thou wert buried underneath an oak
It were the goodliest tree in Christendom.

STEPHANIO 'Tis a fine cargo of guts.

ANGULO   That is as plain
As that two straight lines can't enclose a space,
The angles of his elbows and his knees
And all the other angles of his person
Are all obtuse.   Good living hath worn down
Their natural acuteness.   Both his haunches
Are as the segments of a circle.

BENEDICT   Faugh!

ANGULO And each particular hair upon his scull
Makes up the shortest distance 'tween two points.*

BENEDICT Avaunt! the upright shall not soil his
speech
To answer to th' ungodly.

STEPHANIO   Ay, is't so?
Then, Master Benedict, d'ye hear, bring to,
Unless thy weighty flanks desire bombardment,
Although, i' faith, good Nature gave thy carcase
Broadside enough.   But, rot me, once for all
Drink or be d—d.

BENEDICT   The righteous were made
To suffer persecution.

STEPHANIO   Drink on—

BENEDICT   Hush!
Blast not my hearing with thine obscene oaths.
Sooner than listen to them, I, by drinking,

---

* *I.e.* are combed exactly straight upon his forehead.
This is the definition which Archimedes gives of a straight
line.—A. T.

Will do a violence unto my nature—
Not that I love the carnal taste of wine,
For the Lord knows I'll only wet my lips
That I may stop your execrations.

[*Drinks off the bumper*

ANTONIO Bravo! take heed, he only wets his lips!

PHARMACEUTUS A little wine in moderation
Doth brace the nerves and lend the flagging spirits
A healthful tonic and decent gaiety.

ANTONIO Would it could brace thy person.

PHARMACEUTUS   Or mend thy temper.

ANTONIO Make thy hips firmer.

PHARMACEUTUS   Or thy tongue less voluble.

DEVIL Fie, Gentlemen, no brawls!

STEPHANIO   Fair Excellence,
Thou hast held out long enough. I prithee now
Capitulate on honourable terms,
Disclose the dazzling windows of thine eyes,
Display the rosy banners of thy cheeks,
And open the port cullis of thy lips,
Within whose crimson tenement are rang'd
Thine ivory files of teeth. Consider, prithee,
How shall the airy ardent kiss make way
Through the thick folds of that dark veil, which
  bars
All access to the fortress of thy soul.

ANTONIO Ay! Ay! unveil.

ANGULO   Disperse thy 'nebulæ.'

DEVIL Ay and the *nebulones** that surround me.

ANTONIO Thou wert not used to such reservedness—

* *Nebulones*—Latin word meaning idle rascals.—ED.

50

Veil versus BEAUTY is a case which will
Admit of many pleadings.

DEVIL   'Troth, I dare not
Unveil lest ye should quarrel for my nose.
(*Aside*) (No fear of that methinks) and make parti-
tion
Of all the other features of my face.

ANGULO And think you that we would bisect your
visage?

ANTONIO Will you not face us?

DEVIL   Nay, I cannot countenance ye.

ANTONIO Prithee unveil! why, only double-faces
Do lurk beneath a veil.

DEVIL   And said I not
You wish'd to halve my physiognomy?
You hint that I am double-faced and hence
'Tis plain you wish that half my face were off.

ANGULO Equals from equals taken remain equals.

DEVIL Let me have no divisions on the point.

ANGULO A point hath neither parts nor magnitude,
Thy face hath both and therefore is no point.

DEVIL From thine own wit I judge thy wit is
pointless,
For thou hast parts and therefore lackest point.

ANTONIO How should his inability proceed
From his ability? If he hath parts
Then is he not without ability,
But if his language hath no point in it,
Then his ability is null and void.

ANGULO Which is absurd.

ANTONIO   Can'st solve it?

ANGULO   I say still
    A point hath neither parts nor magnitude—

DEVIL But this is size-point and hath parts and magni-
    tude.

ANTONIO Thou art as full of point as a woolcard,
    Amoret.

DEVIL But you are 'contre-point' and meet me half-
    way.

CAMPANO The devil take discussion—that bears
    point-blank.

STEPHANO I wish the *point* were *doubled*.

ANTONIO   Nay, i' faith
    We've had enough on't.

                  [*Here* BENEDICT *helps himself*
                       What, old Confidence,
    Thou top and Pink of all Morality,
    Thy taste improves then. Marry, but I had
    Some shrewd suspicion that that demi-circle
    Of entrails was bow'd out with better stuff
    Than herb and biscuit.

BENEDICT A—avaunt I—I will not heed the un-
    righteous.

ANTONIO Thou dost not like the *carnal* taste of
    wine?

ANGULO How the saint reels about his centre of
    ɑvity,
    ˌpine subtends an arc of ninety degrees.

STEPHANO 'Faith he hath no small matter in his
    hold,
    He'd keep both pumps at work, I warrant him.

DEVIL I pray ye, Gentlemen, give ear to me,
    It is my wish that e'er I do unveil

The ineffable magic of my charms, that each
In turn should chaunt some love lorn madrigal
Some amorous ditty which may give him scope
To laud with Love's exaggeration
Unto the height of his ability
My loveliness of feature: after which
To him whose strains are sweetest and whose praise
Sounds softest to the ear of vanity
I purpose the unveiling of my beauty
And will admit him to snatch as many kisses
From lips, cheeks, eyebrows, forehead as he wish
Ad libitum. Doth it hit your fancies?

ANTONIO   Ay!
Certes, fair Amoret: Shall I begin?
My voice is sweeter than the chink of silver.

CAMPANO Mine louder than the bugles' clamour.

ANGULO   And mine
Falls with more regular cadence than—

STEPHANIO   And mine's
Like any cannon.

DEVIL   What saith Benedict?

BENEDICT My voice was ever yet employed in
    psalmody.

PHARMACEUTUS But mine—

ANTONIO What! thine! the clicking of thy tongue
Upon thy worn-out palate doth resemble
The livelong hammering of thy cursed pestle
Upon the druggéd mortar and doth surfeit
Our hearing, as thy physicks do our taste.

DEVIL Antonio, prithee sing first.

ANTONIO   Why, then, here goes!
By Jove, I'll warble like the captive thrush.

Thou hast cast over me the golden net,
The all subduing trammels of strong love.
My soul is held in such sweet thrall by thee
Had I the power I would not grant it bail,
Therefore, sweet Excellence, my strains shall be
Most like the imprison'd linnet's.

DEVIL   Prithee, gaol-bird,
No prelude to thy warblings—quick—dispatch.

STEPHANIO I can roar out a catch with th' best o' ye.

ANTONIO If thou presumest to exalt thy voice—

STEPHANIO Avast! Avast there messmate! Anchor
    quietly.
What! do you bear against me? Put about ship
Or ere a hand can reef the mizzen top-sail,
I'll lend thy stern so warm a cannonading
As peradventure, man, may make thy bowsprit
Drip with salt water.

DEVIL   What, Stephanio,
Would'st print the booted fury of thy five toes
Into his yielding carcase?

STEPHANIO   Marry, would I.

PHARMACEUTUS (*whispering* STEPHANIO)
Ay, do't, Stephanio, prithee, do it now.
He lacketh salutary chastisement.

ANTONIO Thou woulds't not meddle sure with my
    entailments.

CAMPANO How! woulds't thou violate his back
    settlements?

STEPHANIO What! do you *side* with him? do you
    back him?

CAMPANO   No,
    Not his back-side.

54

ANTONIO   If thou but stirrest one finger
    Or look'st upon me commandingly—thus,
    I'll let more light into thy skull than ever
    Shone there of nature, with as rude a polt*
    As ever cudgel-swinging bumpkin lent
    His blue and batter'd brother-labourer.
ANGULO There will be 'Vulgar Fractions' then, me-
        thinks.
ANTONIO So! So! you thrust your tongue into your
        cheek
    As if you doubt my prowess—Why, come on then!
    Dost think a lawyer hath but legal weapons?
    Can'st toddle to the scratch? I'll sew your sees up!
    I'll Chancery your upper tenements.
    I'll file and bore you scientifically.
    I'll make the patchwork peep, I warrant you,
    Disorganise your victualling-office, uncork
    The claret of your nob, and dim your daylights,
    And make your ivories chatter in the tusk-box.
STEPHANIO I'll bring my guns to bear on ye enow,
    I'm only gathering wind before I crowd sail.
ANTONIO Ay, ay, for every mugger thou shalt give
        me,
    I'll lend thee ten and ten and ten to that.
ANGULO Oh! a recurring decimal.
STEPHANIO   Come, unrig.
ANTONIO I am your man.
DEVIL (*coming behind*)
                And I your woman, Sir. (*Trips him up*)
ANGULO Quod erat demonstrandum!

* "Polt "—meaning a hard blow, used by Miss Burney in
"Cecilia" and in Jervas' "Don Quixote."—ED.

55

STEPHANIO   Ha! Ha! founder'd!

CAMPANO He hath received some damage in his
     rear,

     And total rout unto his advanc'd guard.

ANTONIO How now! the devil! Amoret!

DEVIL   The Devil's Amoret

     Is a good part if done in character.

     The Devil Amoret! the Devil, Sir!

     I was an Angel twenty minutes since,

     Did I not say that you would change your humour?

ANTONIO Assault and battery!

DEVIL   Ha! Ha! Ha! Antonio,

     And would you swear me in to keep the peace?

PHARMACEUTUS It was a bad concussion. Shall I
     bleed you?

ANTONIO I am bedevil'd and bewizarded.

DEVIL And have you not the grace to say 'bewitched'?

ANTONIO Methought a Giant grappled me—What
     spells

     Have put such thew and sinew in an arm

     Whose rounded purity seem'd only able

     To string a necklace or to clasp a bracelet?

DEVIL What! have I tickled you? your nose drops
     blood.

STEPHANIO How! hath he sprung a leak? hath he
     bilg'd?

ANGULO   He hath prov'd

     The law of gravitation lustily—

     And yet, methought, the vacuum in his skull

     Might have buoyed up his carcase to some purpose.

STEPHANIO He pitches bravely.

ANTONIO   Murrain take ye all!

56

Am I a shrovetide cock that ye should crack
Your jests upon me thus? but I'll not stand it.
DEVIL No, 'faith, you measur'd all your length just
    now.
ANTONIO What do ye take me for?
ANGULO   A baffled lawyer
Diverging from the perpendicular
Which you have done before now—
BENEDICT   Yea, by 'r Lady,
He hath swerv'd from rectitude.
ANTONIO   O chattering Apes,
Do ye make mouths at me? do ye snap your fingers
As ye esteem'd me less than th' heated air
Whose rarefied attenuated substance
Would scarce endure the thistle beard to sport
Upon its yielding subtlety? then, here's for ye,
I value not a single soul among ye
The interest which one poor farthing yields
I' th' fraction of a second.
ANGULO How!
CAMPANO   What!
STEPHANIO Do you brave us all?
ANTONIO   Ay.
STEPHANIO   Split my—
DEVIL   Hist!
                           [*Knocking*
ANTONIO O Lord, the Necromancer!
BENEDICT   Holy Virgin
Defend us!
ANTONIO   We shall all be cats or foxes.
STEPHANIO 'Twill blow a rough gale.
                          [*Knocking*

BENEDICT   Saints deliver me!
   I'll never do an evil thing again.
ANTONIO I'll never nim* a client of his due.
PHARMACEUTUS I'll never kill a patient any more.
STEPHANIO Would I were safe i' my hammock, out
      at sea!
PHARMACEUTUS Would I were mixing draughts
      or rolling pills.
DEVIL Wishes prove nothing but the vanity
      Of him that wisheth: though, like telescopes,
      They bring far things awhile beneath the view,
      They cannot 'minish the long interval
      And space between the object and the wish.
                                             [*Knocking*
      Quick, quick, be expeditious, Gentlemen.
      Look ere you leap but tarry not in looking,
      Were a good proverb.
      A quick decision i' the nick of time
      Outruns mature deliberation
      As the strong gush o' th' tide in some strait river
      Precurses the more sober ocean.
      You mount the chimney, Benedict—what now!
      Do you stick fast in't? doth its sooty breath
      Offend thy proud olfactories? Up farther,
      My ghostly chimney-sweep. I warrant this
      Is not the first time you have made a chimney
      The medium of intrigue. Up farther yet,
      Work thy way inward. Hark ye! Pharmaceutus,
      Stow your long body cheek by jowl with Angulo
      Within the closet yonder. You, Campano,

   "Nim"—used in seventeenth-century slang, meaning
"steal."   Here used to mean "rob."—ED.

58

Cower down beneath the heap o' musty sacks
There i' the corner with Stephanio.
You i' this chest, my worthy Counsellor,
Must with contracted stomach chafe your knees.
So! So! ye are all safe now.
                    [*Loud and continued knocking*
                         I prithee, patience.

SCENE II *Outside of the cottage—early morning.*
MAGUS I do much fear my Devil hath play'd false
     Or that the weeds of wanton Idleness
     Have mantled his clear wit. Why comes he not?
     There is no punishment too sharp for him
     That doth forsake his trust, betray the station
     Where we have set him in Authority.
     If the frail reed we lean upon should break,
     Where most we hope its succour, it were meet
     That we should hew it from the wholesome Earth
     Which nourisheth and perfects better things.
     If he should answer my suspicions,
     I'll pen him for some centuries in ice
     Up to the neck, I'll rack his thumbs with screws;
     I'll twitch his tail until the black blood spout
     Forth at the end; I'll fill his jaws with tooth-ache;
     I'll stick hot pins thro's liver—Hark! he comes.
                         [*Enter* DEVIL, *still veil'd*
     Ha! Amoret, awake, abroad so early
     Blanching the roses of thy cheeks. What now!
     The grey cock hath not crow'd, the glow-worm still
     Leads on unpal'd his train of emerald light.
DEVIL Good faith, most venerable necromancer,
     The roses of my visage are not blanch'd

But rather have attain'd (be thou my judge)
Unto a depth of dusky colouring. (*Unveils*)

MAGUS How now, my Hellish Minister, dark child
Of bottomless Hades; what rude waggery
What jejune undigested joke is this?
To quilt thy fuscous haunches with the flounc'd,
Frilled, finical delicacy of female dress.
How hast thou dar'd to girdle thy brown sides
And prop thy monstrous vertebræ with stays?
Speak out, thou petticoated Solecism.
Thou hairy trifler! what mad pranks have sent
Thy diabolical wits a wool-gathering?

DEVIL A linen gathering I grant you, Master.

MAGUS Certes, it seems your Devilship to-night
Is unaccountably facetious!
Speak and beware the magic of my spells!
Or I will rive yon mighty Cedar-Tree
Sheer from its topmost windiest branch unto
The lowest fang o' th' root—between each half
I'll place thy sinful carcase and again
When the cleft stem shall close without a fissure
Thy bunching body shall be quash'd as flat
As spider in a hinge.

DEVIL   Nay, prithee—

MAGUS   Speak, then,
And tell me why thy horny scalp is thus
Envelop'd in the foldings of this veil?

DEVIL Why lurks the Bravo's dagger in the sheath
Ere yet it glitter o'er his enemy?
Why is the curvéd fish-hook buried in
The length o' th' twisting worm? My gudgeons
   play

Around the baited snare. My horny scalp
Is buried in the foldings of this veil
To save thy scalp from horns.

MAGUS   Ay? is it so?
Good Devil bear with me. My nature is
Most quickly mov'd to anger which as quickly
Is wasted like the flint o' th' veiny Earth
Which underneath the hoof one moment flashes
A particle of intense fire which dies
As instantly. But wind and wave have chafed me,
The Anarchy of the impetuous blast
And the wet beatings of the step-dame surge
Have ruffled my smooth temper.

DEVIL   Gentle Master,
Unless thine oars had been swift wings, thy boat
Some pinion'd steed of air, thine ocean-path
The limitless abyss of Ether's space,
I know not how thou hast measur'd back thy way
So keenly.

MAGUS   Half the powers o' th' other world
Were leagued against my journeying: but had not
The irresistible and lawless might
Of brazen-handed fix'd Fatality
Oppos'd me, I had done it. The black storm,
From out whose mass of volum'd vapour sprang
The lively curling thunderbolt had ceas'd
Long ere from out the dewy depth of Pines
Emerging on the hollow'd banks, that bound
The leapings of the saucy tide, I stood—
The mighty waste of moaning waters lay
So goldenly in moonlight, whose clear lamp
With its long line of vibratory lustre

61

Trembled on the dun surface, that my Spirit
Was buoyant with rejoicings. Each hoar wave
With crisped undulation arching rose,
Thence falling in white ridge with sinuous slope
Dash'd headlong to the shore and spread along
The sands its tender fringe of creamy spray.
Thereat my shallop lightly I unbound,
Spread my white sail and rode exulting on
The placid murmurings of each feathery wave
That hurried into sparkles round the cleaving
Of my dark Prow; but scarcely had I past
The third white line of breakers when a squall
Fell on me from the North, an inky Congress
O' the Republican clouds unto the zenith
Rush'd from th' horizon upwards with the speed
Of their own thunder-bolts.
The seas divided and dim Phantasies
Came thronging thickly round me, with hot eyes
Unutterable things came flitting by me;
Semblance of palpability was in them,
Albeit the wavering lightnings glitter'd thro'
Their shadow'd immaterialities.
Black shapes clung to my boat; a sullen owl
Perch'd on the Prow, and overhead the hum
As of infernal Spirits in mid Heaven
Holding aerial council caught mine ear.
Then came a band of melancholy sprites,
White as their shrouds and motionlessly pale
Like some young Ashwood when the argent Moon
Looks in upon its many silver stems.
And thrice my name was syllabled i' th' air
And thrice upon the wave, like that loud voice

Which thro' the deep dark night i' th' olden time
Came sounding o'er the lone Ionian.
Thereat I girded round my loins the scarf
Thy Mother Hecate gave me and withstood
The violent tempest: the insulting surge
Rode over me in glassy arch but dar'd not
Sprinkle one drop of its nefarious spray
Upon my charméd person: the red heralds
O' th' heavy footed thunder glanc'd beside me,
Kiss'd my bar'd front and curl'd around my brow
In lambent wreaths of circling fire, but could not
Singe one loose lock of vagrant grey, that floated
To the wind's dalliance. But nor magic spells
Vigour of heart or vigilance of hand,
Could back the Ocean's spumy menacings,
Which drove my leaky skiff upon the sands.
Soon as I touch'd firm Earth, each mounting billow
Fell laxly back into its windless bed,
And all the moon-lit Ocean slumber'd still.
Thrice with bold prow I breasted the rough spume
But thrice a vitreous wall of waves up sprung
Ridging the level sea—so far'd it with me
Foil'd of my purpose. Some unwholesome star,
Some spells of darker Gramarie than mine,
Rul'd the dim night and would not grant me
    passage.
DEVIL Thou hast come fittingly.
MAGUS   How so?
DEVIL   My plans
    Are growing to a head.
MAGUS   And hast thou guarded
    With scrupulous exactness—

63

DEVIL   Grant me but
The tenth part of an hour and I will mesh
In the entanglement of stratagem
These lawless insolents; thyself shall take
That vengeance which thou wishest.
MAGUS   Who are within?
DEVIL Water and oil.
MAGUS   What mean you?
DEVIL   Salt and pepper.
MAGUS Be less ambiguous.
DEVIL   A most warring compound
Of uncongenial elements, good Master.
'Faith, seldom doth thy dice box, Intercourse,
Turn up such rude unmated numbers.
MAGUS   Ha!
Where's Amoret?
DEVIL   Asleep.
MAGUS   Art sure?
DEVIL   Most certain.
MAGUS 'Tis well. I wait without. What signal, prithee,
Shall summon my approach?
DEVIL   A beat o' th' foot, or
The shrill collision of my palms—thus—thrice, or
A clearing of the throat—thus—meaningly.
MAGUS I will be sure to mark it. Get thee gone
And do thy bidding, Devil.

                                   [*Exit* DEVIL
                       'Tis even thus—
And they would pluck from th' casket the sole gem
Of mine affections, taint its innocent lustre,
And give it back dishonour'd, they would canker
My brightest flower, would muddy the clear source

                       64

Whence flows my only stream of earthly bliss;
Would let the foul consuming worm into
The garner of my love. O Earthliness!
Man clambers over the high battlements
That part the principalities of good
And ill—perchance a few hot tears, and then
The sear'd heart yields to 't and Crime's signet
    stamps
Her burning image there. The summer fly
That skims the surface of the deep black pool
Knows not the gulf beneath its slippery path.
Man sees, but plunges madly into it.
We follow thro' a night of crime and care
The voice of soft Temptation, still it calls,
And still we follow onwards, till we find
She is a Phantom and—we follow still.
When couched in Boyhood's passionless tranquillity,
The natural mind of man is warm and yielding,
Fit to receive the best impressions,
But raise it to the atmosphere of manhood
And the rude breath of dissipation
Will harden it to stone. 'Tis like the seaplant
Which in its parent and unshaken depths
Is mouldable as clay, but when rude hands
Have pluck'd it from its billowless Abyss
Unto the breathings of Heaven's airs, each gust
Which blows upon 't will fix it into hardness.
I'll to the Northern casement which looks over
The shrubby banks o'th' mountain Lake, for thence
The slightest whisper from within may reach me.

SCENE III *Interior of* MAGUS' *cottage. Enter*
     DEVIL.
DEVIL O ye puissant spirits whose tried powers
     The issue of this night hath fully prov'd,
     Though your undoubted prowess hath descended
     In dearth of other merriment to play
     At hide and seek—come forth!
STEPHANIO (*Whispering from under his sacks.*)
                                   Is the coast clear?
     Has he heel'd offward?
ANTONIO (*Half raising the lid of the chest.*)
                              Is the sorcerer gone?
DEVIL 'Awake, arise, or be for ever fallen.'
CAMPANO What! did he beat a parley with thee,
     Amoret?
     Or did ye sally forth, and nail his Ordnance
     Ere it had vent?
BENEDICT (*Up in the chimney.*)
                              The Lord deliver me!
     That ever Benedict should come to this!
DEVIL Out of your holes, ye Rats! uncavern ye,
     White-liver'd conies!
ANTONIO   Why, thou art a Shrew.
DEVIL Nay, give the Devil his due, I am not shrewish.
ANTONIO Beshrew me, if thou art not. Where is
     Magus,
     And his familiar?
DEVIL   Fear, like Drunkenness
     Sees ever double—there was only one.
     'Twas an old suitor whom I had discarded,
     A miserly craving man, whose white hairs preach
     Against his manners,
                              66

One who hath heap'd up coin until the means
Became the end of being; his hair was lac'd
With cobwebs, his sad calculating brows
Gather'd into a hundred dusty wrinkles.
A rusty key with many less ones dangled
Beside him, his parch'd person showed most like
A disembowell'd Mummy or dried Moth.
There was no moisture in his fissur'd lip.
He thrust his shrivell'd fingers into mine,
And mumbled from his dry and corky tongue
Some sentences which intimated Love,
But sounded like chaf'd parchment or the whistle
Of tight and corded Inexpressibles.*
Ev'n such an one so sapless and so wither'd
I clos'd my door upon.

BENEDICT (*Groaning in the chimney*)
                                        Beate Martin!

ANTONIO He calls for Betty Martin.

DEVIL   And he'll find her
    For she is marvellously fond of soot.

PHARMACEUTUS (*Who has advanced into the stage
        with* ANGULO.)
    Did you speak verity, my oil of Roses?
    Who shook the door so keenly?

ANGULO   Ay, good mistress,
    Are we correct i' th' data?

DEVIL   Know you not
    Philargyrus, to whose roof the sparrow's nest
    Owes not a straw that lines it?

* I suggest, with some diffidence, that this line refers to
the whistling sound which is caused by the rubbing together
of the legs of corduroy trousers in walking.—ED.

PHARMACEUTUS Know him? Ay,
    A weak, old patient with a thready pulse,
    And dry unfruitful palm, which lacketh ever
    The wholesome dew of perspiration.
    But I much marvel how he knocked so briskly.
DEVIL He was enrag'd we did not open to him:
    And irritation often times doth nerve
    The puny frame with artificial strength.
    A child in wrath will cast a heavy stone,
    Which in his tamer mood he scarce had mov'd.
    But to the point! We tarry long in colloquy,
    The cool and pearly grey of dawn hath crept
    Into the sable bosom of the night.
    It were fit time that I should call from ye
    The man that hits my fancy.
PHARMACEUTUS Wilt unveil then,
    My liniment of Linseed, my Electuary,*
    My syrup of Poppies, eh? my flower of sulphur?
DEVIL (*Aside*) That's a *home* touch, though but a
        random hit.
    My flower of sulphur quotha! by the Cabbala
    A pretty flower of sulphur shall ye find me.
    My thoughts begin to burn: a Devil's heat
    Glows through me to the core: have at ye, Sirs!

Here the manuscript ends abruptly.—ED.

* "Electuary"—a medical paste made of some powder or
other ingredient mixed with honey or syrup.—ED.

UNPUBLISHED EARLY POEMS

PREFACE

THE poems contained in this volume were never published by Tennyson, or, with one exception to which I will refer later, by his son, Hallam Lord Tennyson, in whose possession the MS. of them remained until his death in 1928. He left them, with other MSS., to me with liberty to publish at my discretion.

The great majority of the poems date from the poet's boyhood and his residence at Cambridge, and I have divided the material into three sections, headed respectively "Boyhood," "Cambridge Period," and "1830–1842."

The first two sections are very much the most important, and in these I have included one poem ("The Coach of Death") which was published by Hallam Tennyson in his Memoir of the poet, in order to gather into one volume all the very remarkable Juvenilia which are not to be found in the authorised editions of Tennyson's works.

"The Devil and the Lady," which was issued by Messrs. Macmillan in February 1930, gave the world convincing evidence of Tennyson's precocity. This play, written when the poet was only fourteen years old, is a brilliant experiment in the vein of the Elizabethan comedy, showing a command of versification, a richness of language and imagery, a vivacity of humour and a range of knowledge which are positively astounding. The translation from Claudian's "Proserpine" in rhyming heroic verse, which is the first poem in this volume, is an equally brilliant experiment, imitative, of course, but with a spirit and vivacity which are all its own.

Imitative, too, is "Armageddon," probably written in the poet's fifteenth or sixteenth year. This fragment, which was the foundation of Tennyson's Prize Poem "Timbuctoo," is strictly Miltonic, both in subject and technique, but, like the other early poems, has a vigour and imaginative power (and sometimes an unconscious humour) of its own. These experiments show that Tennyson, like most if not all fine artists, founded his greatness on an intensive study and imitation of the work of his great predecessors. There is little originality of form, though all give evidence of highly individual powers of observation, emotion and fancy. As the boy passes through adolescence, the note becomes more personal. "The Coach of Death" is an experiment in the *macabre*, which gives a foretaste of the "Vision of Sin," published nearly twenty years later. The ode "O Bosky Brook," though over-elaborate and involved in form and expression, foreshadows the nature poetry which was so strong a feature of Tennyson's mature work. In "Perdidi Diem" sound the notes of doubt and gloom which animate the "Supposed Confessions" and "The Two Voices." These boyish poems have an ingenuous vigour and charm which are very attractive. The work of the Cambridge Period shows a much greater freedom of handling and control of form, and the variety and freshness of subject and technique make it easy to understand the tremendous impression which Tennyson's verse made upon his contemporaries at the University. It is interesting to note that several of the poems of this time exist not only in Tennyson's hand-writing but in copies made by others, no doubt for circulation amongst his friends.

Of special interest is the fragment "Ilion, Ilion." This poem, with the "Hesperides" (printed in the notes to the Eversley Edition, Vol. 1, p. 326), shows a classicism which has no doubt grown out of the "Rape of Proserpine," but has been transmuted into something new and golden. It was to be still further sublimated in the "Lotos-Eaters," "Oenone," "Ulysses," and "Tithonus."

So, too, with the Blank Verse. This has passed from the Shakespearean exercise of "The Devil and the Lady," through the Miltonics of "Armageddon" to a freer and richer style (which, however, still shows traces of Milton and Shakespeare) in the lines "Working High Treason." These lead up to the "Lover's Tale," which was written in 1831–32, and represent a further stage in the evolution of a verse flexible and rich enough to achieve "Oenone," "The Gardener's Daughter," and the "Morte D'Arthur." A similar development, though along a line which Tennyson never carried further, is that from the rhymed couplets of the Proserpine fragment to those which begin and end the "Vision of Sin," published twenty years later. In these twenty years the couplet has passed from the mechanical brilliance and regularity characteristic of the eighteenth century to a freedom and trochaic lightness which make it almost unrecognisable. These are the only two examples of rhymed heroic verse in Tennyson's published work, though there exists in MS. in the Library of Trinity College, Cambridge, a poem in this metre, on the retreat of Napoleon from Moscow, which seems to represent an intermediate style. There are, unfortunately, no traces of any early experiments leading up to the wonderful Spenserian stanzas of the "Lotos-Eaters," Tennyson's only extant attempt at that historic form. It is remarkable, having regard to his early admiration for Spenser, Thomson and Byron, that no trace of an apprenticeship to Spenser's great stanza survives.

Mention may also be made of the collection of sonnets, all but one apparently written in the poet's nineteenth and twentieth years. Tennyson is commonly held to have failed in this form. Many of these sonnets, though imperfect in finish, seem to me superior to most of those in the published works and suggest that, had the poet cared to persevere with this form of composition, he would have become a master of the art. The number of different rhyme schemes employed is remarkable. Of the ten sonnets printed only two have similar arrangements; only one is on the true Italian model; one normal Shakespearean, and the remainder all more or less irregular.

Something should perhaps be said of the poems entitled "Marion," "Lisette," and "Amy," which recall "Lilian," "Rosalind," "Eleanore," etc., in the volumes of 1830 and 1832. These early poems have been adversely criticised, often with little discrimination. They are the work of a very young man, and some of them no doubt are inferior; but I do not think anyone who reads (for example) "Rosalind" or "Eleanore" without prejudice can fail to realise that they show great metrical skill and have considerable beauty. They are, however, the outcome of an attitude towards women which is antipathetic and appears rather ridiculous to modern ideas, and this prevents them from being read without prejudice.

The three poems which I have included seem to me to have very genuine merits.

Finally, I will mention one curious characteristic of Tennyson's methods of composition of which various examples occur in this volume. I have noted in these early poems a number of lines which the poet used again, often years afterwards, in quite different contexts, in his published work. It is known and has been remarked that Tennyson often stored observations and similes for long periods before finally working them into his poems, and this storage of actual lines from early compositions is a fresh illustration of the same tendency. The remarkable thing is that the lines, when finally taken from storage, fit so naturally and aptly into their new context that they are often among the best passages in the poems in which they are employed.

So far I have dwelt chiefly on the historical value of the earlier verses which, with "The Devil and the Lady," form a unique record of a great poet's adolescence. But this is not the volume's only interest. I do not believe that any lover of poetry will doubt that its contents deserve to be published on their merits. The fact that Tennyson himself did not publish them during his long life is intelligible, though in some cases surprising. With his hatred of personal publicity, he would be the last person to do anything which would look like calling attention to his own incredible precocity, by the publication of early and immature work. Moreover, many of the poems are fragments or were for some reason never brought to the degree of perfection on which his fastidious taste insisted. While the poet was alive and able to bring his work to perfection, he was not likely to issue anything imperfect. Now that this is no longer possible, the only valid reason for withholding publication disappears.

It remains to add that the poems are printed exactly as Tennyson left them except for the omission of one or two obviously imperfect passages and some modifications of punctuation and the use of capital letters, particularly in the earlier pieces.

Parts of the "Rape of Proserpine" and "Armageddon" and all the other poems included in the volume, with the exception of "The Coach of Death," "In Deep and Solemn Dreams," "Sense and Conscience" and "The Outcast," appeared in *The Nineteenth Century and After* (issues for March, April and May 1931).

I am indebted to the Trustees of the late Hallam Lord Tennyson for permission to include "The Coach of Death."

C. T.

CONTENTS

xiii

PART I
BOYHOOD

TRANSLATION FROM CLAUDIAN'S
"PROSERPINE"

T H E gloomy chariot of the God of night,
And the wan stars that sicken'd at the sight,
And the dark nuptials of th' infernal King,
With senses rapt in holy thought, I sing.
Away! away! profane ones! ye whose days
Are spent in endless sin and error's maze,
Seraphic transports through my bosom roll,
All Phoebus fills my heart and fires my soul.
Lo! the shrines tremble and a heavenly light
Streams from their vaulted roofs serenely bright,
The God! the God, appears! the yawning ground
Moans at the view, the temples quake around,
And high in air the Eleusinians raise
The sacred torch with undulating blaze;
Hiss the green snakes to sacred rapture giv'n
And meekly lift their scaly necks to heav'n,
With easy lapse they win their gentle way
And rear their rosy crests and listen to my lay.
See! see! where triform Hecate dimly stands,
And mild Iacchus leads the tuneful bands!
Immortal glories round his temples shine,
And flow'ring ivy wreaths his brows entwine;
From Parthia's land he clasps beneath his chin
The speckled honours of the tiger's skin;
A vine-clad thyrsus with celestial grace
Sustains his reeling feet and props his falling pace.

B   I

Ye mighty demons, whose tremendous sway
The shadowy tribes of airy ghosts obey,
To whose insatiate portion ever fall
All things that perish on this earthly ball,
Whom livid Styx with lurid torrent bounds
And fiery Phlegethon for aye surrounds,
Dark, deep and whirling round his flaming caves
The braying vortex of his breathless waves,
Eternal spirits! to your bard explain
The dread Arcana of the Stygian reign,
How that stern Deity, Infernal Jove,
First felt the power, and own'd the force of love;
How Hell's fair Empress first was snatch'd away
From Earth's bright regions, and the face of day;
How anxious Ceres wander'd far and near
Now torn by grief and tortur'd now by fear,
Whence laws to man are giv'n, and acorns yield
To the rich produce of the golden field.
Hell's haughty Lord in times of old began
To rouse 'gainst Heav'n the terrors of his clan;
Stern fury shook his soul—that he alone
Of every God upon his glitt'ring throne,
Should lead a dull and melancholy life,
Without the fond endearments of a wife—
Wretch that he was, who knew not how to claim
A consort's or a father's dearer name!
Now Hell's misshapen monsters rush to arms
And fill the wide abyss with loud alarms;
The haggard train of midnight Furies meet
To shake the Thunderer from his starry seat,
And pale Tisiphone, with baleful breath
Calls the thin Ghosts within the camp of Death;

2

High in her hand amid the shades of night
The gleaming pine shoots forth a dismal light,
Around her head the snaky volumes rise
And dart their tongues of flame and roll their gory eyes.
Now had all nature gone to wrack again
And Earth's fell offspring burst their brazen chain,
And from the deep recesses where they lay
Uprisen in wrath to view the beam of day,
Now had the fierce Aegaeon thrown aside
The adamantine limits of his pride,
Uprear'd his hundred-handed form on high
And dar'd the forkéd terrors of the sky;
But the dire Parcae with a piercing yell
Before the throne of gloomy Pluto fell,
Around his knees their suppliant hands were thrown,
Those awful hands which make the world their own,
Whose dreadful power the shades of Hades fear
And men on earth, and Gods in Heav'n revere,
Which mark the lot of fate's unerring page
And ply their iron tasks through every age.
First Lachesis began (while all around
Hell's hollow caverns shudder'd at the sound),
"Dark Power of night and God of Hell, for whom
We draw the fated threads of human doom,
Thou end and origin of all on earth,
Redeeming death below by human birth!
Thou Lord of life and dissolution! King
Of all that live! (for first from thee they spring
And to thee they return, and in thy reign
Take other shapes and seek the world again)
Break not, ah! break not with unholy deed
That peace our laws have fix'd, our threats decreed.

3

Oh, wake not thou the trumpet's impious swell
Nor raise thy standard in the gulph of Hell
Nor rouse the Titans from their dread abode,
The hideous Titans, foes to man and God.
Jove,—Jove himself shall grant thine ardent wish
And some fond wife shall crown thy nuptial bliss."
She spake—the God was struck with sudden shame
And his wild fury lost its former flame.
So when with whirlwinds in his icy train
Stern Boreas sweeps along the sounding plain,
Bright o'er his wings the glittering frost is spread
And deathless winters crown his hoary head,
Then bow the groves, the woods his breath obey,
The heaving Ocean tosses either way.
But lo! if chance on far Aeolia's shores
The God of winds should close his brazen doors,
With sudden pause the jarring tumults cease,
And Earth, Air, Ocean, find one common peace.
Then Maia's son he calls, in haste to bear
His fix'd commands through all the deep of air;
Prompt at the word Cyllenius is at hand
Adorn'd with pinion'd brow and magic wand.
Himself the God of terrors, rear'd on high,
Sits thron'd in shades of midnight majesty,
Dim wreaths of mist his mighty sceptre shroud,
He veils his horrors in a viewless cloud.
Then thus in haughty tone the God began
(Through Hell's wide halls the echoing accents ran,
The bellowing beast that guards the gates of Hell
Repress'd the thunder of his triple yell,
And sad Cocytus at the sudden cry
Recall'd his wailing stream of misery.

4

From Acheron's banks no sullen murmurs spread,
His hoarse waves slumbered on his noiseless bed,
'Gan Phlegethon in surly haste retire
And still his whirling waves and check his flood of fire),
"Grandson of Atlas, thou whose footsteps stray
Through Hell's deep shadows, and the realms of day,
To whom alone of all the Gods 'tis giv'n
To tread the shores of Styx and halls of Heav'n,
Chain of each world and link of either sphere,
Whom Tegea's sons in silent awe revere,
Go, cleave the winds and bear my will to Jove,
That haughty God who sways the realms above. . . .

Note.—This is a free translation into 133 English lines of the
first 93 lines of Claudian's "De Raptu Proserpinae."

The MS. of this fragment is in the same notebook as that of the
earliest version of "The Devil and the Lady," which it precedes.
The title-page of the notebook is inscribed "Translation of Claudian's Proserpine, by A. Tennyson," and bears no reference to "The
Devil and the Lady," so that the Claudian translation is evidently
the earlier poem of the two, and the earliest extant poem by Tennyson. He himself said that he wrote "hundreds and hundreds of
lines in the regular Popeian metre," after reading Pope's "Iliad,"
which was a favourite book of his when he was about eleven or
twelve.

The first draft of "The Devil and the Lady" was written when
he was fourteen (see the Preface to the edition published by
Macmillan & Co. in February 1930), and this translation, therefore, belongs to a period between the eleventh and fourteenth years
of the poet.

The Latin text of Claudian's lines is included in an appendix to
this volume.

ARMAGEDDON

(MS.
obliterated
here.—C.T.
.................................Prophecy whose mighty grasp
...........................ings whose capacious soul
.................................illimitable abyss
...............................bottomless futurity
...........................giant figures that shall pace
....................of its stage—whose subtle ken
....................the doubly darkened firmament
.....................to come with all its burning stars
.....................erful intervals. I thank thy power,
Whose wondrous emanation hath poured
Bright light on what was darkest, and removed
The cloud that from my mortal faculties
Barred out the knowledge of the Latter Times.

I stood upon the mountain which o'erlooks
The valley of destruction and I saw
Things strange, surpassing wonder; but to give
Utterance to things unutterable, to paint
In dignity of language suitable
The majesty of what I then beheld,
Were past the power of man. No fabled Muse
Could breathe into my soul such influence
Of her seraphic nature, as to express
Deeds inexpressible by loftiest rhyme.

I stood upon the mountain which o'erlooks
The valley of Megiddo.—Broad before me

6

Lay a huge plain whereon the wandering eye,
Weary with gazing, found no resting-place,
Unbroken by the ridge of mound or hill
Or far-off cone of some aerial mount
Varying the horizon's sameness.

                         Eve came down
Upon the valleys and the sun was setting;
Never set sun with such portentous glare
Since he arose on that gay morn, when Earth
First drunk the light of his prolific ray.
Strange figures thickly thronged his burning orb,
Spirits of discord seem'd to weave across
His fiery disk a web of bloody haze,
Thro' whose reticulations struggled forth
His ineffectual, intercepted beams,
Curtaining in one dark terrific pall
Of dun-red light heaven's azure and earth's green.

  The beasts fled to their dens; the little birds
All wing'd their way home shrieking: fitful gusts
Of violent tempest shook the scanty palm
That cloth'd the mountain ridge whereon I stood:
And in the red and murky Even light,
Black, formless, unclean things came flitting by;
Some seemed of bestial similitude
And some half human, yet so horrible,
So shadowy, indistinct and undefin'd,
It were a mockery to call them ought
Save unrealities, which took the form
And fashioning of such ill-omened things
That it were sin almost to look on them.

There was a mingling too of such strange sounds
(Which came at times upon my startled hearing)
Half wailing and half laughter; such a dissonance
Of jarring confus'd voices, part of which
Seem'd hellish and part heavenly, whisperings,
Low chauntings, strangled screams, and other notes
Which I may liken unto nothing which
I ever heard on Earth, but seem'd most like
A mixture of the voice of man and beast;
And then again throughout the lurid waste
Of air, a breathless stillness reigned, so deep,
So deathlike, so appalling, that I shrunk
Into myself again, and almost wish'd
For the recurrence of those deadly sounds,
Which fix'd my senses into stone, and drove
The buoyant life-drops back into my heart.

Nor did the glittering of white wings escape
My notice far within the East, which caught
Ruddy reflection from the ensanguin'd West;
Nor, ever and anon, the shrill clear sound
Of some aerial trumpet, solemnly
Pealing throughout the Empyrean void.

Thus to some wakeful hind who on the heights
Outwatches the wan planet, comes the sound
Of some far horn along the distant hills
Echoing, in some beleaguer'd country, where
The pitiless Enemy by night hath made
Sudden incursion and unsafe inroad.

The streams, whose imperceptible advance
Lingering in slow meanders, once was wont

8

To fertilize the plain beneath—whose course
Was barely mark'd save by the lazy straws
That wandered down them—now, as instinct with life,
Ran like the lightning's wing, and dash'd upon
The curvature of their green banks a wreath
Of lengthen'd foam; and yet, although they rush'd
Incalculably swift and fring'd with spray
The pointed crags, whose wave-worn slippery height
Parted their glassy channels, there awoke
No murmurs round them—but their sapphire depths
Of light were changed to crimson, as the sky
Glow'd like a fiery furnace.
                              In the East
Broad rose the moon, first like a beacon flame
Seen on the far horizon's utmost verge,
Or red eruption from the fissur'd cone
Of Cotopaxi's cloud-cap't altitude;
Then with dilated orb and mark'd with lines
Of mazy red athwart her shadowy face,
Sickly, as though her secret eyes beheld
Witchcrafts, abominations, and the spells
Of sorcerers, what time they summon up
From out the stilly chambers of the earth
Obscene, inutterable phantasies.

    The sun went down; the hot and feverish night
Succeeded; but the parch'd, unwholesome air
Was unrecruited by the tears of heaven.
There was a windless calm, a dismal pause,
A dreary interval, wherein I held
My breath and heard the beatings of my heart.
The moon show'd clearer yet, with deadlier gleam,

Her ridgéd and uneven surface stain'd
With crosses, fiery streaks, and wandering lines—
Bloody impressions! and a star or two
Peer'd through the thick and smoky atmosphere.

Strange was that lunar light: the rock which stood
Fronting her sanguine ray, seem'd chang'd unto
A pillar of crimson, while the other half
Averted, and whatever else around
Stood not in opposition to her beams,
Was shrouded in the densest pall of night
And darkness almost palpable.
                                        Deep fear
And trembling came upon me, when I saw
In the remotest chambers of the East
Ranges of silver tents beside the moon,
Clear, but at distance so ineffable,
That save when keenly view'd, they else might seem
But little shining points or galaxies,
The blending of the beams of many stars.

Full opposite within the lurid West,
In clear relief against the long rich vein
Of melancholy red that fring'd the sky,
A suite of dark pavilions met mine eyes,
That covered half the western tide of Heaven,
Far stretching, in the midst of which tower'd one
Pre-eminent, which bore aloft in air
A standard, round whose staff a mighty snake
Twin'd his black folds, the while his ardent crest
And glossy neck were swaying to and fro.

The rustling of white wings! The bright descent
Of a young seraph! and he stood beside me
In the wide foldings of his argent robes
There on the ridge, and look'd into my face
With his unutterable shining eyes,
So that with hasty motion I did veil
My vision with both hands, and saw before me
Such coloured spots as dance before the eyes
Of those that gaze upon the noonday sun.

"O Son of Man, why stand you here alone
Upon the mountain, knowing not the things
Which will be, and the gathering of the nations
Unto the mighty battle of the Lord?
Thy sense is clogg'd with dull Mortality,
Thy spirit fetter'd with the bond of clay—
Open thine eyes and see!"
      I look'd, but not
Upon his face, for it was wonderful
With its exceeding brightness, and the light
Of the great Angel Mind that look'd from out
The starry glowing of his restless eyes.
I felt my soul grow godlike, and my spirit
With supernatural excitation bound
Within me, and my mental eye grew large
With such a vast circumference of thought,
That, in my vanity, I seem'd to stand
Upon the outward verge and bound alone
Of God's omniscience. Each failing sense,
As with a momentary flash of light,

Grew thrillingly distinct and keen. I saw
The smallest grain that dappled the dark Earth,
The indistinctest atom in deep air,
The Moon's white cities, and the opal width
Of her small, glowing lakes, her silver heights
Unvisited with dew of vagrant cloud,
And the unsounded, undescended depth
Of her black hollows. Nay—the hum of men
Or other things talking in unknown tongues,
And notes of busy Life in distant worlds,
Beat, like a far wave, on my anxious ear.

I wondered with deep wonder at myself:
My mind seem'd wing'd with knowledge and the
        strength
Of holy musings and immense Ideas,
Even to Infinitude. All sense of Time
And Being and Place was swallowed up and lost
Within a victory of boundless thought.
I was a part of the Unchangeable,
A scintillation of Eternal Mind,
Remix'd and burning with its parent fire.
Yea! in that hour I could have fallen down
Before my own strong soul and worshipp'd it.

Highly and holily the Angel look'd.
Immeasurable Solicitude and Awe,
And solemn Adoration and high Faith,
Were trac'd on his imperishable front—
Then with a mournful and ineffable smile,
Which but to look on for a moment fill'd
My eyes with irresistible sweet tears,

In accents of majestic melody,
Like a swollen river's gushings in still night
Mingled with floating music, thus he spoke.

III

"O Everlasting God, and thou not less
The Everlasting Man (since that great spirit
Which permeates and informs thine inward sense,
Though limited in action, capable
Of the extreme of knowledge—whether join'd
Unto thee in conception or confin'd
From former wanderings in other shapes
I know not—deathless as its God's own life,
Burns on with inextinguishable strength),
O Lords of Earth and Tyrannies of Hell,
And thrones of Heaven, whose triple pride shall clash
In the annihilating anarchy
Of unimaginable war, a day
Of darkness riseth on ye, a thick day,
Pall'd with dun wreaths of dusky fight, a day
Of many thunders and confuséd noise,
Of bloody grapplings in the interval
Of the opposéd Battle, a great day
Of wonderful revealings and vast sights
And inconceivable visions, such as yet
Have never shone into the heart of Man—
THE DAY of the Lord God!"
                              His voice grew deep
With volumes of strong sound, which made the rock
To throb beneath me, and his parted locks
Of spiral light fell raylike, as he mov'd,

On each white shoulder: his ambrosial lip
Was beautifully curv'd, as in the pride
And power of his mid Prophecy: his nostril
Dilated with Expression; half upturn'd
The broad beneficence of his clear brow
Into the smoky sky; his sunlike eyes
With tenfold glory lit; his mighty arm
Outstretch'd described half-circles; small thin flashes
Of intense lustre followed it.

IV

                    I look'd,
And lo! the vision of the night was chang'd.
The sooty mantle of infernal smoke
Whose blank, obliterating, dewless cloud
Had made the plain like some vast crater, rose
Distinct from Earth and gather'd to itself
In one dense, dry, interminable mass
Sailing far Northward, as it were the shadow
Of this round Planet cast upon the face
Of the bleak air. But this was wonderful,
To see how full it was of living things,
Strange shapings, and anomalies of Hell,
And dusky faces, and protruded arms
Of hairy strength, and white and garish eyes,
And silent intertwisted thunderbolts,
Wreathing and sparkling restlessly like snakes
Within their grassy depths. I watch'd it till
Its latest margin sank beneath the sweep
Of the horizon.

All the crimson streaks
And bloody dapplings faded from the disk
Of the immaculate morn.

                An icy veil
Of pale, weak, lifeless, thin, unnatural blue
Wrapt up the rich varieties of things
In grim and ghastly sameness.

                   The clear stars
Shone out with keen but fix'd intensity,
All-silence, looking steadfast consciousness
Upon the dark and windy waste of Earth.
There was a beating in the atmosphere,
An indefinable pulsation
Inaudible to outward sense, but felt
Thro' the deep heart of every living thing,
As if the great soul of the Universe
Heav'd with tumultuous throbbings on the vast
Suspense of some grand issue. . . .

Note.—When Tennyson was in his second year at Cambridge, his father pressed him to enter for the Prize Poem (the "Chancellor's Medal"). He consented, though much against his will. The subject of the competition was "Timbuctoo," and Tennyson, apparently unwilling to devote much thought or labour to the task, sent home for this early poem on the somewhat incongruous theme of "Armageddon," which he adapted to the subject in hand. The poem won the prize, in spite of the fact that it was in blank verse instead of the rhyming couplet, which was still regarded as the only fitting metre for a prize poem, and in spite of an obscurity and lack of form which was no doubt partly due to the method of its composition.

"Armageddon" is evidently very early work and this is probably an early draft, seeming from the handwriting to have been written when the poet was not more than fifteen. "Timbuctoo" was published in the Oxford University Press "Tennyson," edited by Sir T. Herbert Warren, and a comparison of the two poems shows that only a very small quantity of "Armageddon" was actually incorporated in "Timbuctoo," though there is a similarity between the general framework of the poems. In each an angel comes down to the poet when standing on a mountain.

"Timbuctoo" commences with the line—

"I stood upon the mountain which o'erlooks," which begins the second and third paragraphs of "Armageddon," though in the former poem the mountain overlooks not Megiddo but the Straits of Gibraltar. Then follow sixty lines in which the poet dreams of the legend of lost Atlantis, and asks if Africa still holds a city;

> " as fair
> As those which starr'd the night o' the Elder World?
> Or is the rumour of thy Timbuctoo
> A dream as frail as those of ancient times?"

Then comes the next similarity (cf. the opening lines of Part II of "Armageddon"):

> "A curve of whitening, flashing, ebbing light!
> A rustling of white wings! The bright descent
> Of a young seraph! And he stood beside me
> There on the ridge, and look'd into my face
> With his unutterable, shining orbs."

The seraph is then described in lines which do not occur in the earlier poem and asks the poet why he muses on these old legends and bids him open his eyes and see. Then follow the twenty-four lines from Armageddon which begin:

> " I look'd, but not upon his face,"

and end:

> " Beat like a far wave on my anxious ear,"

which are perhaps the best lines in both poems, and of interest as being a very early description by the poet of the mystical experience of separation of spirit from body, which he believed that he experienced from time to time (cf. "The Ancient Sage" and the early poem "The Mystic" quoted in the notes on that poem in the collected edition).

In "Timbuctoo" Tennyson inserted six new lines after

> " of her black hollows."

in the twenty-first line, and omitted the next fifteen lines of this fine passage, the only remaining similarity to "Armageddon" being the subsequent incorporation in quite a different context of the last six lines of Part II.

THE COACH OF DEATH[1]

(A fragment)

F A R off in the dun, dark Occident,
　Behind the burning Sun:
Where his gilding ray is never sent,
　And his hot steeds never run:

There lies a land of chilling storms,
　A region void of light,
A land of thin faces and shadowy forms,
　Of vapors, and mist, and night.

There never green thing will gaily spring
　In that unwholesome air,
But the rickety blast runs shrilly and fast
　Thro' the bony branches there.

When the shadow of night's eternal wings
　Envelopes the gloomy whole,
And the mutter of deep-mouth'd thunderings
　Shakes all the starless pole,

Thick sobs and short shrill screams arise
　Along the sunless waste,
And the things of past days with their horrible eyes
　Look out from the cloudy vast.

---

[1] Published by Hallam Lord Tennyson in his Memoir (see p. 23, one-volume edn.), and stated to have been written by the poet at fourteen or fifteen years of age (*ib.* p. 19).

And the earth is dry, tho' the pall of the sky
  Leave never an inch of blue;
And the moaning wind before it drives
  Thick wreaths of cloudy dew.

Whoever walks that bitter ground
  His limbs beneath him fail;
His heart throbs thick, his brain reels sick:
  His brow is clammy and pale.

But some have hearts that in them burn
  With power and promise high,
To draw strange comfort from the earth,
  Strange beauties from the sky.

———————

Dark was the night, and loud the roar
  Of wind and mingled shower,
When there stood a dark coach at an old Inn door
  At the solemn midnight hour.

That Inn was built at the birth of Time:
  The walls of lava rose,
Cemented with the burning slime
  Which from Asphaltus flows.

No sound of joy, no revelling tones
  Of carouse were heard within:
But the rusty sign of a skull and cross-bones
  Swung creaking before the Inn.

No taper's light look'd out on the night,
  But ever and anon

Strange fiery eyes glared fiercely thro'
    The windows of shaven bone.

And the host came forth, and stood alone
    And still in the dark doorway:
There was not a tinge on each high cheek bone
    But his face was a yellow gray.

The skin hung lax on his long thin hands;
    No jolly host was he;
For his shanks were shrunken to willow wands
    And his name was Atrophy!

Dimly the travellers look'd thro' the glooms,
    Worn and wan was their gaze, I trow,
As the shrivell'd forms of the shadowy grooms
    Yoked the skeleton horses to.

They lifted their eyes to the dead, pale skies,
    And above the barkless trees
They saw the green verge of the pleasant earth,
    And heard the roar of her seas.

They see the light of their blest firesides,
    They hear each household voice:
The whisper'd love of the fair young wives;
    And the laugh of their rose-lipp'd boys.

The summer plains with their shining leaves,
    The summer hills they see;
The dark vine leaves round the rustling eaves,
    And the forests, fair and free.

———————

19

There came a gaunt man from the dark Inn door,
   A dreadnought coat had he:
His bones crack'd loud, as he stept thro' the crowd,
   And his boots creak'd heavily.

Before his eyes so grim and calm
   The tingling blood grew chill,
As each put a farthing into his palm,
   To drive them where he will.

His sockets were eyeless, but in them slept
   A red infernal glow;
As the cockroach crept, and the white fly leapt
   About his hairless brow.

They mounted slow in their long black cloaks,
   The tears bedimm'd their sight;
The grim old coachee strode to the box,
   And the guard gasp'd out "All's right."

The leaders bounded, the guard's horn sounded:
   Far away thro' the night ran the lengthen'd tones:
As the quick wheels brush'd, and threw up the dust
   Of dead men's pulverised bones.

Whose blood in its liveliest course would not pause
   At the strife of the shadowy wheels,
The chattering of the fleshless jaws,
   And the beat of the horny heels?

Deep dells of snow sunk on each side below
   The highway, broad and flat,

20

As the coach ran on, and the sallow lights shone
    Dimly and blurly with simmering fat.

Vast wastes of starless glooms were spread
    Around in the chilling air,
And heads without bodies and shapes without heads
    Went leaping here and there.

O Coachee, Coachee, what lights approach
    With heavenly melodies?
Oh! those are the lights of the Paradise coach,
    That so gaily meet their eyes!

With pleasant hymns they soothe the air
    Of death, with songs of pride:
With sackbut, and with dulcimer,
    With psaltery they ride.

These fear not the mists of unwholesome damps
    That through that region rove,
For all wreath'd with green bays were the gorgeous
        lamps,
    And a bright archangel drove.

They pass'd (an inner spirit fed
    Their ever-burning fires,)
With a solemn burst of thrilling light,
    And a sound of stringéd lyres.

With a silver sound the wheels went round,
    The wheels of burning flame;
Of beryl, and of amethyst
    Was the spiritual frame.

Their steeds were strong exceedingly:
    And rich was their attire:
Before them flow'd a fiery stream;
    They broke the ground with hoofs of fire.

They glitter'd with a stedfast light,
    The happy spirits within;
As stars they shone, in raiment white,
    And free from taint of sin.

ODE: O BOSKY BROOK

O B O S K Y brook, which I have lov'd to trace
Thro' all thy green and winding ways,
Wandering in the pure light of youthful days
　　Along yon dusky windy hills,
Whose dark indent and wild variety
Curtails the Southern sky,
Following, thro' many a windy grove of pines,
White undergrowth of hemlock and hoar lines
Of sallows, whitening to the fitful breeze,
　　The voiceful influx of thy tangled rills—
How happy were the fresh and'dewy years
　　When by thy damp and rushy side,
　　In the deep yellow Eventide,
I wept sweet tears,
Watching the red hour of the dying Sun,
And felt my mind dilate
With solemn uncontrollable pleasure, when
The sad curve of the hueless Moon,
Sole in her state,
Varied with steadfast shades the glimmering plain,
And full of lovely light
Appear'd the mountain tarn's unbroken sleep,
Which never felt the dewy sweep
Of oars, but blackly lay
Beneath the sunny living noon,
Most like an insulated part of night,
Tho' fair by night as day:

So deep, that when day's manhood wears his crown
Of hottest rays in Heaven's windy Hall,
To one who pryeth curiously down,
From underneath the infathomable pall
    And pressure of the upright wave,
The abiding eyes of Space, from forth the grave
    Of that black Element,
Shine out like wonderful gleams
    Of thrilling and mysterious beauty, sent
From gay shapes sparkling thro' the gloom of
    dreams.

II

Well have I known thee, whatsoe'er thy phase,
In every time and place,
Pale Priestess of grey Night,
Whether thy flood of mournful rays,
Parted by dewless point of conic hill,
Adown its richer side
    Fell straying
Into the varied valley underneath;
Or where, within the eddying tide
Of some tumultuous mountain rill,
Like some delusive charm
Thy mimic form,
Full opposite to thy reality,
    Broken and flashing and playing
In tremulous darts of slender light,
Beguiled the sight;
Or on the screaming waste of desolate heath
In midnight full of sound,

24

Or in close pastures soft as dewy sleep,
Or in the hollow deep
Of woods, whose counterchang'd embroidery
Of light and darkness chequered the old moss
On the damp ground;
Or whether thou becamest the bright boss
    Of thine own Halo's dusky shield,[1]
        Or when thou burnest beaconlike upon
    The margin of the dun and dappled field
        Of vagrant waves, or higher ris'n, dost link
        Thy reflex to the steadfast brink,
    With such a lustrous chord of solemn sheen,
That the heart vibrates with desire to pace
The palpitating track of buoyant rays;
    Or when the loud sea gambols and the spray
Of its confliction shoots and spreads and falls,
Blossoming round the everduring walls
            Which build up the giant cape,
            Whose mass'd and wonder-stirring shape
                And jutting head,
[2] Citadel-crowned and tempest-buffeted,
Runs far away,
(What time the white West glows with sickening ray)
And in the middle ocean meets the surging shock,
And plumes with snowy sheen each gather'd crest,
The lighthouse glowing from the secret rock,
The seabird piping on the wild salt waste.

[1] Cf. Stanza IV of "The Voyage," published in 1864.
[2] The line "Tempest-buffeted, citadel-crowned" occurs in the poem "Will" published in 1855.

III

I savour of the Egyptian and adore
Thee, venerable dark! august obscure!
     Sublimest Athor!
   It is not that I doat upon
      Thy glooms, because the weary mind is
       fraught
   With fond comparison
Of thy deep shadow to its inward strife,
     But rather,
      That as thou wert the parent of all life,
E'en so thou art the mother of all thought,
Which wells not freely from the mind's recess
    When the sharp sunlight occupies the sense
With this fair world's exceeding comeliness,
    The goodly show and varied excellence
    Of lithe tall trees, the languor of sweet flowers
      Into the universal herbage woven,
       High hills and broad fair vallies river-cloven,
   Part strown with lordly cities and with towers,
Part spotted with the gliding white of pregnant sails;
Add murmur, which the buxom gales
     (As my glowing brows they fan)
       Bear upward thro' the happy heights
        of air,
       Chirp, bellow, bark and distant shout of
        man—
       Not that the mind is edged,
       Not that the spirit of thought is freshlier
        fledged

With stillness like the stillness of the tomb
And grossest gloom,
As it were of the inner sepulchre.
Rare sound, spare light will best address
The soul for awful muse and solemn watchfulness. . . .

Note.—This fragment is evidently of early origin. A preliminary and less complete version exists in a notebook which contains some very early verses, apparently of about the date of "The Devil and the Lady" (written *aetat.* fourteen). The fragment is in three somewhat disconnected parts. The first is addressed to a brook, not the famous Holywell brook, though no doubt the description is, in parts, reminiscent of it, but to an imaginary mountain stream. The second is addressed to the moon, the last to darkness.

THE OUTCAST

I W I L L not seek my father's groves,
They murmur deeply o'er my head
Of sunless days and broken loves:
Their shade is dim and dark and dead.
There thro' the length of cool arcades,
Where noonday leaves the midnight dews,
Unreal shapes of twilight shades
Along the sombre avenues,
To Memory's widowed eyes would spring
In dreamy, drowsy wandering.

I will not seek my father's hills,
Their hue is fresh and clear and bright,
What time the early sunbeam fills
Their bush-clad depths with lonely light.
Each broken stile, each wavy path,
Each hollowed,hawthorn, damp and black,
Each brook that chatters noisy wrath
Among its knotted reeds, bring back
Lone images of varied pain
To this worn mind and fevered brain.

I will not seek my father's hall:
There peers the day's unhallow'd glare,
The wet moss crusts the parting wall,
The wassail wind is reveller there.
Along the weedy, chinky floors

Wild knots of flowering rushes blow
And through the sounding corridors
The sere leaf rustles to and fro:
And oh! what memory might recall
If once I paced that voiceless Hall!

Note.—The MS. (not in Tennyson's hand) is initialled "A.T.
1826." The lines, therefore, date from the poet's seventeenth
year.

IN DEEP AND SOLEMN DREAMS

I N deep and solemn dreams I view
Great cities by an ocean blue,
Terrace upon terrace bright
Standing out in sunny light,

And sheeny spires and turrets mixt
With pomp of burnish'd domes betwixt,
And pinnacles, and airy halls
With fairy fretwork on the walls,

And rows of pillars high and light,
That end in lines of streaky white,
Brooded o'er by dovelike rest,
Like a City of the Blest.

All adown the busy ways
Come sunny faces of lost days,
Long to mouldering dust consign'd,
Forms which live but in the mind.

Then methinks they stop and stand,
And I take each by the hand,
And we speak as we have spoken
Ere our love by death was broken.

With tearless ageless eyes that glisten
In light and tranquil mirth, they listen,
And as sleep the brain beguiles
Smile their old familiar smiles.

But ere long that silent sea,
Rising wild and wrathfully,
Sweeps in all-embracing might
Friends and city from my sight—
Then I lie and toss and mourn
Hopeless, heartless and forlorn.

Then I dream again, and lo!
Round me press a laughing row,
A careless, free and happy crowd,
With merry hearts and voices loud,
On the level sungirt lawn
Ere the glorious sun be born.

And I gaze without a tear
On their countenances clear,
On their noble foreheads white,
And their eyes divine with light—

"Hark away! 'tis early morn,
The East is crimson to the dawn,
We have waked the matin bird
And the brooks may yet be heard.

Brothers, come ! the twilight's tears
Are heavy on the barley spears,
And the sweet winds tremble o'er
The large leaves of the sycamore.[1]

[1] Cf.   IN MEMORIAM XCV.

And sucked from out the distant gloom
    A breeze began to tremble o'er
    The large leaves of the sycamore,
And fluctuate all the still perfume,

Hark away ! we'll weave to-day
A garland of all flowers gay,
Where the freshest flowers be
To the far wood walks will we."

Yet a little, brothers, keep
The sacred charm of tearless sleep—
Oh unkind ! what darkening change
Hath made your features dim and strange !

Dear lips, loved eyes, ye fade, ye fly,
Even in my fear ye die,
And the hollow dark I dread
Closes round my friendless head,

And far away, to left and right,
Whirlwinds waste the dizzy night,
And I lie and toss and mourn,
Hopeless, heartless and forlorn.

Note.—There are several extant versions of this poem, which
seems to have been begun at Somersby and finished at Cambridge.

MEMORY

A y me! those childish lispings roll
As thunder thro' my heart and soul,
Those fair eyes in my inmost frame
Are subtle shafts of pierceant flame.

Blessèd, cursèd, Memory,
Shadow, Spirit as thou may'st be,
Why hast thou become to me
A conscience dropping tears of fire
On the heart, which vain desire
Vexeth all too bitterly?
When the wand of circumstance
All at once hath bid thee glance,
From the body of the Past,
Like a wandering ghost aghast,
Why wearest thou, mad Memory,
Lip and lip and hair and eye,[1]
Life—life without life or breath,
Death forth issuing from Death?

May goes not before dark December,
Nor doth the year change suddenly ;
Wherefore do I so remember
That Hope is born of Memory
Nightly in the house of dreams?
But when I wake, at once she seems

[1] The first word of this line is very hard to decipher and I cannot
guarantee the text.

The faery changeling wan Despair,
Who laughs all day and never speaks—
O dark of bright! O foul of fair!
A frightful child with shrivelled cheeks.

Why at break of cheerful day
Doth my spirit faint away
Like a wanderer in the night?
Why in visions of the night
Am I shaken with delight
Like a lark at dawn of day?
As a hungry serpent coiled
Round a palm tree in the wild,
When his bakéd jaws are bare
Burning in the burning air,
And his corky tongue is black
With the raging famine-crack,
If perchance afar he sees
Winding up among the trees,
Lordly-headed buffaloes,
Or but hears their distant lows,
With the fierce remembrance drunk
He crushes all the stalwart trunk
Round which his fainting folds are prest,
With delirium-causing throes
Of anticipated zest.

Note.—This fragment, which is very hastily written, occurs in the same notebook as the two preceding poems, "O Bosky Brook" and "In Deep and Solemn Dreams." It, too, appears to belong to the Somersby–Cambridge transition period.

PERDIDI DIEM

A N D thou hast lost a day! Oh mighty boast!
Dost thou miss one day only? I have lost
A life, perchance an immortality;
I never *liv'd* a day, but daily die,
    I have no real breath;
My being is a vacant worthlessness,
A carcase in the coffin of this flesh,
    Pierc'd thro' with loathly worms of utter Death.
My soul is but th' eternal mystic lamp,
Lighting that charnel damp,
Wounding with dreadful days that solid gloom,
And shadowing forth th' unutterable tomb,
Making a 'darkness visible'
Of that which without thee we had not felt
As darkness, dark ourselves and loving night,
Night-bats into the filtering crevices
Hook'd, clinging, darkness-fed, at ease:
Night-owls whose organs were not made for light.
I must needs pore upon the mysteries
Of my own infinite Nature and torment
My Spirit with a fruitless discontent:
As in the malignant light
Of a dim, dripping, moon-enfolding night,
Young ravens fallen from their cherishing nest
On the elm-summit, flutter in agony
With a continual cry
About its roots, and fluttering trail and spoil

Their new plumes on the misty soil,
But not the more for this
Shall the loved mother minister
Aerial food, and to their wonted rest
Win them upon the topmost branch in air
With sleep-compelling down of her most glossy breast.
In chill discomfort still they cry—
What is the death of life if this be not to die?

II

You tell me that to me a Power is given,
An effluence of serenest fire from Heaven,
Pure, vapourless, and white,
As God himself in kind, a spirit-guiding light,
Fed from each self-originating spring
Of most inviolate Godhead, issuing
From underneath the shuddering stairs which climb
The throne,
Where each intense pulsation
And going-on o' th' heart of God's great life,
Out of the sphere of Time,
As from an actual centre is heard to beat,
And to the thrilling mass communicate,
Goes through and through with musical fire and
    through
The spiritual nerves and arteries
Of those first spirits, which round the incorruptible
    base
Bow, with furl'd pinions veiling their immortal eyes,
As not enduring, face to face,
Eye-combat with th' unutterable gaze.

36

These are the highest few:
Thence to the lower, broader circle runs
The sovran subtil impulse on and on,
Until all Heaven, an inconceivable cone
Of vision-shadowing vans and claspéd palms,
Of circle below circle, file below
File, one life, one heart, one glow,
Even to the latest range which tramples on the highest
    suns,
With every infinite pulsation
Brightens and darkens; downward, downward still
The mighty pulses thrill
With wreathéd light and sound,
Thro' the rare web-work woven round
The highest spheres,
Prompting the audible growth of great harmonious
    years.
Base of the cone,
Last of the link,
Each rolling sun and hornéd moon,
All the awful and surpassing lights
Which we from every zone
Of th' orbed Earth survey on summer nights,
(When nights are deepest and most clear)
Are in their station cold;
The latest energies of light they drink:
The latest fiat of Divine Art,
Our Planets, slumbering in their swiftness, hear
The last beat of the thunder of God's heart. . . .

Note.—This fragment is from a notebook inscribed "A. Tennyson, Trin: Coll:, Cambridge." An earlier version of the first few
lines also exists, suggesting that the lines were begun at Somersby.

PART II
CAMBRIDGE

PLAYFELLOW WINDS

P L A Y F E L L O W winds and stars, my friends of old,
    (For sure your voice was friendly, your eyes bright
    With sympathy, what time my spirit was cold
    And frozen at the fountain, my cheek white
As my own hope's quench'd ashes) as your memories
    More than yourselves you look, so overcast
    With steam of this dull Town your burning eyes:
Now surely e'en your memories wear more light
Than do your present selves. Ye sympathise
As ever with me, stars, from first to last.

Note.—These lines are from a notebook inscribed "A. Tennyson, Trin. Coll. Camb." A copy also exists, written in another
hand and dated 1827. It was more probably written in 1828, in a
mood of depression during the poet's first days at Cambridge.

SENSE AND CONSCIENCE

W O R K I N G high Treason toward thy sovranty,
A traitorous and unfaithful minister,
Have I been lavish of thy treasures, Time.
Thy stores were shallow enow, but on their briefness
Have I drawn largely and often, hoping they
Were deeper than I found them, ill-informed,
An ignorant vain steward: they lie so thin now
I cannot choose but see their shallowness.
When they are wasted I am out of place,
And that must needs come quickly: for I have not
(As the condition of mine office ran)
Used them to furnish necessary wars
With fitting front of opposition,
And subtil temperament of harden'd arms,
Wherewith to embattail *Spirit*, whose fair ranks,
Strong in their essence but undisciplin'd,
Were shock'd and riv'n and shaken asunder wide,
And ridden over by the exulting *Sense*,
Their clamorous shrieks dust-stifled—

                         Rather, Time,
Unto the abuse of thy most precious ore,
Did I win over the Arch-Enemy *Sense*,
And set him in the chiefest offices
And heights of the State, unto the infinite rack
Of those few faithful in the land, which still
Cried out against my stewardship. Then Sense
Grew large and prosper'd at the court of Time,

Say rather, took away all thought of Time
By his own imminent greatness, and then first
Made me his bondsman, and by violence
Wrench'd from my grasp the golden keys which guard
The doors o' the Treasure-house. Great Conscience
    then,
The boldest of the warriors of Time,
Prime mover of those wars of Spirit and Sense,
The wisest of the councillors of Time,
Ere while my bosom friend, whose voice till now
Was loudest in the Council-room against
The prevalent Ministry, was drugg'd to sleep
By a most stealthy potion given by Sense—
To *sleep !* for neither edge of finest steel
Nor barbéd fire of spears, nor deadliest draught
Could drive him to the death: such subtlety
Of revivescence in his spirit lay,
Infus'd by his immortal Parentage,
Reason and Will !
                They drove him to deep shades,
A gloom monotonously musical
With hum of murmurous bees, which brooded deep
In ever-trembling flowers, and constant moan
Of waterfalls i' th' distance, and low winds
Wandering close to Earth, and voice of doves,
Which ever bowing cooed and cooing bowed
Unto each other as they could not cease.
Long time he lay and slept: his awful brows
Pillow'd on violet-woven mosses deep;
The irrepressible power of his keen eyes
Burn'd thro' the shadow of their down-dropt lids;
One hand was flung to distance; the barr'd iron

Of battle-writhen sinews crush'd and mass'd
The pleasurable flowers; the other grasp'd
The hilt of that great blade of puissant flame
Hight the *heart-cleaver*.

                        Alway in his sight
Delicious dreams floated unto the music
Of winds (whose fragrance and whose melodies
Made sweet contention which should sweeter be,
And thro' contention grew to perfectness
Of most inviolate communion),
And witching fantasies which won the heart,
Lovely with bright black eyes and long black hair
And lips which moved in silence, shaping words
With meaning all too sweet for sound.

                                 At last
Came Memory wandering from afar, with stern
Sad eyes and temples wan cinctur'd with yew;
Pain went before her alway half turn'd round
To meet her coming with drawn brows low-bent
Whetting a dart on which her tears fell ever,
Softening the stone that she might point the steel.
The Giant rais'd his eyes and saw and knew
The blackness of her shadow where she stood
Between him and the moonlight of his soul.
He started to his feet, but lacking strength
From so long sleep fell prone, and tears of fire
Wept, filling all the joyous flower-cups
With burning blight and odour-quenching sighs,
So that their golden colours fell away
O'er-flown with pale. Rage seiz'd upon him then
And grasping with both palms his wondrous blade,
Sheer through the summit of the tallest flowers

He drave it: the rose fell, the argent lily,
The dappled fox-glove with its poison'd leaves,
And the tall poppy fell, whose eminent flower,
Hued with the crimson of a fierce sunrise,
Like to the wild youth of an evil King
Is without sweetness, but who crowns himself
Above the secret poisons of his heart
In his old age. The ivy from the stem
Was torn, the vine made desolate; his feet
Were crimson'd with its blood, from which flows joy
And bitterness, first joy from bitterness,
And then again great bitterness from joy.
Soon shrouding with his hand his guilty eyes,
Into the heart of the realm afar he fled
And lived on little roots which memory
Dug for him round his cell.
                                        One solemn night
He could not sleep, but on the bed of thorns,
Which Memory and Pain had strown for him,
Of brambles and wild thistles of the wood,
Lay tossing, hating light and loathing dark,
And in his agony his heart did seem
To send up to his eyes great drops of blood,
Which would not fall because his burning eyes
Did hiss them into drought. Aloud he wept,
Loud did he weep, for now the iron had come
Into his soul: the hollow vaulted caverns
Bore out his heavy sobs to the waste night,
And some the low-browed arch return'd unto
His ear; so sigh from sigh unceasing grew. . . .

Note.—These lines are an unfinished allegory of the struggle
between Sense and Conscience. The giant whose fate is here

described is Conscience; he is drugged by the adherents of Sense and cast out into a remote forest. The poem is contained in a notebook inscribed: "A. Tennyson, Trin: Coll:, Cambridge." The poppy simile was afterwards transplanted to "The Lover's Tale." I have omitted one very involved and obviously imperfect passage of ten lines, the deletion of which causes no interruption of the sense.

"ILION, ILION"

I L I O N, Ilion, dreamy Ilion, pillared Ilion, holy Ilion,
City of Ilion when wilt thou be melody born?
Blue Scamander, yellowing Simois from the heart of
     piny Ida
Everwhirling from the molten snows upon the
     mountainthrone,
Roll Scamander, ripple Simois, ever onward to a
     melody
Manycircled, overflowing thoro' and thoro' the
     flowery level of unbuilt Ilion,
City of Ilion, pillared Ilion, shadowy Ilion, holy Ilion,
   To a music merrily flowing, merrily echoing
   When wilt thou be melody born?

Manygated, heavywalléd, manytowered city of Ilion,
From the silver, lilyflowering meadowlevel
   When wilt thou be melody born?
Ripple onward, echoing Simois,
Ripple ever with a melancholy moaning,
   In the rushes to the dark blue brimméd Ocean,
     yellowing Simois,
To a music from the golden twanging harpwire
     heavily drawn.
   Manygated, heavywalléd, manytowered city of
     Ilion,
   To a music sadly flowing, slowly falling,
   When wilt thou be melody born?

Note.—This fragment is from a pocket-book which contains fragments of many of the poems published in the volume of 1830. It is therefore almost certainly of the Cambridge period. I have retained the compound words which the poet employed at this period but afterwards abandoned, as they seem almost essential to the rhythm.

Tennyson's MS. indicates the syllabic scansion of the first stanza as follows :—

Ilion, Ilion, dreamy Ilion, pillared Ilion, holy Ilion,
City of Ilion when wilt thou be melody born?
Blue Scamander, yellowing Simois from the heart of piny Ida
Everwhirling from the molten snows upon the mountainthrone,
Roll Scamander, ripple Simois ever onward to a melody
Manycircled overflowing thoro' and thoro' the flowery level of
    unbuilt Ilion,
City of Ilion, pillared Ilion, shadowy Ilion, holy Ilion,
    To a music merrily flowing, merrily echoing
    When wilt thou be melody born?

48

ELEGIACS

OVER an old gate leaning i' th' mellow time of the
  gleaning
Pleasant it was to hark unto the merry woodlark,
Loudly he sang from the thicket, and nigher the shrilly
  balm-cricket
Under a full-leaved spray chirruped and carolled
  away.
Under a sky red-copéd the lights of the evening
  slopéd,
All with a roseate heat tipping the points of the wheat;
Every cloud over the dim sun was barred and bridgéd
  with crimson,
Only one great gold star burn'd thro' a cleft from afar.
Over a brook and two meadows beyond, up among the
  elm shadows,
Steeped in the sunlight calm glowed the white walls of
  the farm;
Three full wains had been thither with labour, three
  empty come hither;
Half of the gold stack stared over the pales in the yard.

Note.—These lines come from a notebook inscribed "A. Tennyson, Trin. Coll., Cambridge." They are very roughly written and
entirely without stops. There is a gap in the MS. between lines
eight and nine, which suggests that the poet may have intended to
add another couplet there. The lines may be compared with the
"Leonine Elegiacs" in the 1830 volume.

MARION

T H O U art not handsome, no, nor plain,
   And thou dost own no graceful art,
Thou hast no little winning ways
Whereby to win our love or praise,
    Yet holdest thou an ample reign
      Within the human heart.
It is a sort of pride in thee,
    In every shade of joy or woe
    Still with the general mood to flow,
    Nor more nor less, but ever so.
What is it oversteps this law,
And overshowers the daily and the real
    As with a fruitful rain of grace?
    Let me die, Marion, if I ever saw
    Such ideal unideal,
      Such uncommon commonplace!
Though thought and art and speech in thee
    Run parallel with thought and speech
In the universal Mind,
    My gentle Marion, couldst thou teach
      That peculiar alchemy
    To the rest of womankind,
Which evermore to precious ore
    Changes common thought in thee,
    That spiritual economy,
Which wasteth not itself in signs,
And yet with power intertwines
    Thine image with the memory,

The world would build thee silver shrines.
  From what far inward source
    Is that rare influence drawn,
  Enlightening all intercourse
  With thee, my quiet Marion?
Which can illustrate every nameless act,
  And from the eyelids of hardfeatured fact
  Rain tender starlight on the heart?
That magically woven net
Thou threwest round me when we met,
  Thin-threaded as the cobweb round
In a corner of the glass,
  Wherewith the green-winged moth is bound
  And seeth not and cannot pass.
It is the slow-increased delight
  Of unperceivéd gentleness,
That touching with scarce visible ray
The barren light of every day,
  Possesseth all its nakedness
With stealing shadows dusk and bright.

Love is a vine, and in the hot
  And southern slopes he takes delight;
  He curls his tendrils in thy light,
But his grape clusters ripen not:
But mild affection taketh root
  And prospers in thy placid light.
Thou art the soul of commonplace
  The body all mankind divide.—

Note.—A note in the handwriting of Hallam Lord Tennyson
attributes this poem to the Cambridge period. The last two lines
do not fit into the rhyme scheme, so "Marion" cannot be regarded
as a finished work.

LISETTE

M Y light Lisette
   Is grave and shrewd,
   And half a prude,
And half coquette,
So staid and set,
   So terse and trim,
   So arch and prim
Is my Lisette.

A something settled and precise
Hath made a home in both the eyes
   Of my Lisette,
Lives in the little wilful hands,
   The little foot that glides and flits,
Braced with dark silken sandal-bands,
   Even in the coxcomb parrokette
That on the drooping shoulder sits
   Of trim Lisette.

The measured motion of the blood;
   The words, where each one tells,
Too logical for womanhood,
   Brief changes rung on silver bells;
The cheek with health's close kisses warm,
   The finished form so light;
Such fullness in a little form
   As satisfies the sight;

The bodice fitted so exact;
   The nutbrown tress so crisply curled,
And the whole woman so compact,
   Her match is nowhere in the world;
Such knowledge of the modes of life,
   And household order such,
As might create a perfect wife,
   Not careful overmuch;
      All these so moved me
         When we met,
      I would she loved me,
         Trim Lisette.

What if to-morrow morn I go,
   And in an accent clipt and clear
   Say some three words within her ear,
I think she would not answer "No."
   But by the ribbon in her hair,
   And those untasted lips, I swear,
      I keep some little doubt as yet;
         With such an eye
         So grave and sly,
            Looks my Lisette.
         What words may show
         The "Yes"—the "No"—
            Of trim Lisette?
         The doubt is less,
            Since last we met,
         Let it be "Yes"
            My sweet Lisette.

AMY

HIGHMINDED and pure-thoughted, chaste and
  simple,
  In Life's broad river set
A lily, where the waters faintly dimple,
  Leaving the flower unwet;
The silver tongues of featherfooted rumour
  Ne'er spake of thee to me,
Thou hast no range of wit, no wealth of humour,
  But pure humility
Dwelling like moonlight in a silver vapour;
  Not pale St. Agatha
Bent o'er her missal by her waxen taper,
  Not sweet Cecilia,
St. Agnes on St. Agnes' Eve, who leadeth
  Over the snowy hill
Her snowwhite lambs and with hushed footstep
  treadeth,
  Is not so chaste and still
In the cold moon, e'er yet the crocus flamy
  Or snowdrop burst to life;
Yet with a human love I love thee, Amy,
  And woo thee for my wife. . . .
Dear sainted Amy, thou dost never tremble
  To starts or thrills of love,
But rather in thy motion dost resemble
  Hill-shaded streams, that move
Through the umber glebe and in brown deeps embosom
  The tremulous Evenstar,

Fold within fold thou growest, a virgin blossom,
  In dewy glades afar . . .
Yet take blind Passion; give him eyes; and freeing
  His spirit from his frame
Make double-natured love lose half his being
  In thy spiritual flame,
Till like a rainbow in a rainbow folded
  And of a rainbow made,
My spirit within thy spirit may be moulded,
  My soul of thine the shade.

Note.—These lines are from the same pocket-book as the
"Ilion" fragment in what is apparently a hurried first draft of a poem
which the poet intended to revise. Some lines are very hard to
decipher and I have omitted two passages, which were obviously
very imperfect. So much is necessary to explain the poem's
evident defects, in spite of which I think it has qualities which
justify its publication.

LINES

W H A T are you, lady? Nought is here
  To tell your name or story,
To claim for you our smile or tear,
  To dub you Whig or Tory;
I don't suppose we ever met,
  And how shall I discover
Where first you danced a minuet,
  Or first deceived a lover?

Tell me what day the Post records
  Your mother's silk and satin;
What night your father lulls the Lords
  With little bits of Latin;
Who makes your shoes, whose skill designs
  Your dairy or your grotto;
And in what page Debrett enshrines
  Your pedigree and motto.

And do you sing or do you sigh?
  And have you taste in bonnets?
And do you read philosophy?
  Or do you publish sonnets?
And does your beauty fling away
  The fetters Cupid forges?
Or—are you to be married, pray,
  To-morrow at St. George's?

56

I ceased—methought the pencilled fan
    Fluttered, or seemed to flutter—
Methought the painted lips began
    Unearthly sounds to mutter, . . .
"I have no house, no ancestry,
    No wealth, no reputation;
My name, fair sir, is 'Nobody';
    Am I not your relation?"

Note.—These verses only exist in a series of poems copied in a hand not Tennyson's. The first four lines are almost identical with the opening lines of W. M. Praed's well-known poem "To the Portrait of a Lady in the Exhibition of the Royal Academy" (Everyday Characters).

    "What are you, lady, nought is here
        To tell your name or story,
    To claim the gazer's smile or tear,
        To dub you Whig or damn you Tory,"

but the two poems have no other resemblance, and even the metre differs slightly (in the fourth line of the stanza). According to Derwent Coleridge's edition of Praed (see Vol. II, p. 155) his poem was published in 1831. Here is something of a problem. As, however, all the other poems in the series which includes this poem are (except where expressly stated) by Tennyson, I think this must also be his, in spite of its dissimilarity to his known work and its similarity to Praed's.

The explanation probably is that Tennyson saw the Praed poem when it was published in some periodical in 1831, memorised the first four lines and amused himself by making them the basis of an exercise in Praed's manner.

If this is a true explanation, the lines show with what skill the poet could adopt and reproduce the style of another and very different writer.

SONNET

S H E took the dappled partridge fleckt with blood,
And in her hand the drooping pheasant bare,
And by his feet she held the woolly hare,
And like a master-painting where she stood,
Lookt some new goddess of an English wood.
Nor could I find an imperfection there,
Nor blame the wanton act that showed so fair—
To me whatever freak she plays is good.
Hers is the fairest Life that breathes with breath,
And *their* still plumes and azure eyelids closed
Made quiet Death so beautiful to see
That Death lent grace to Life and Life to Death
And in one image Life and Death reposed,
To make my love an Immortality.

SONNET

ALAS! how weary are my human eyes
   With all the thousand tears of human scorn.
   Alas! how like the dappled moon at morn
My waning spirit after darkness sighs.
Thro' kindling buds hale March will yearly blow
   On hollow winds his gusty showerdrops,
   And many an April sprinkle the blue copse
With snowy sloethorn-flowers when I am low,
And brown September laughing cheerily
   Bruise his gold grain upon his threshing-floor,
And all the infinite variety
   Of the dear world will vary evermore.
      Close weary eyes, breathe out my weary breath,
      One only thought I have, and that is death.

SONNET

SALVE LUX RENATA

H A I L, Light, another time to mortal eyes
    Issuing from behind the starry veil,
How gently morn steals from the misty skies
    Touching dim heights with sheeted radiance pale.
Pleased I behold, for to my inward sight
    Within that dawn there dawns a mystery,
The shining marvel of another light,
    On this auspicious day newborn to me.
Therefore, Oh Lord, whose effluence increate
    Was light from everlasting; who dost call
Each several morn "Let there be light" and strait
    For a day's space the light is over all,
        Grant to my dawn of joy a dawnlight strength
        To lead up into day of summer length.

Note.—This sonnet is obviously, and no doubt deliberately, reminiscent of the Invocation to Light at the beginning of Book III of "Paradise Lost."

SONNET

T H E Wise, the Pure, the lights of our dull clime,
   Fall from the age, and we shall roam the gloom,
   Wild hearts, whom their own rage and heat consume,
Weak wings, that every Sophister can lime.
They will not hear the loud lies of the time
   To come, the shallow fret and frothy fume
   Of brass-mouthed demagogues, O'Connell, Hume,
And the others whom the sacred Muse of rhyme
   Disdains to name. O that true Liberty
Would ride upon the singing winds, and blow
   Her silver trumpet clear from sky to sky,
     That we might see, who love her all in all
For her fair self, and of a surety know
   Those men that to the golden idol fall.

SONNET

W O E to the double-tongued, the land's disease,
   Lords of the hustings, whose mob-rhetoric rends
   The ears of Truth! How shall they make amends,
Those that would shatter England's ancient ease
Built on broad bases and the solid peace
   Wherein she prospered?—Woe to those false friends
   That mouth great things and for their own vile ends
Make swarm with brazen clang the humming bees;
   Those that would turn the ploughshares into swords,
   Those that inflame themselves with idle words
In every market-place. Their doom is signed,
   Tho' they shall cause confusion and the storms
   Of civil blood—Moths, cankers, palmer-worms
That gnaw the bud, blind leaders of the blind.

SONNET

A H, fade not yet from out the green arcades,
   Fade not, sweet Rose, for hark! the woodland shrills,
A lamentation grows in all the shades,
   And grief in copses where the linnet trills:
   The sweet Rose fades from all the winding rills
And waning arches of the golden glades:
   From all the circuit of the purple hills
The sweet Rose fades, alas, how soon it fades.
It does not fade, but from the land it goes,
   And leaves the land to winter. I remain,
      To waste alone the slowly-narrowing days.
It fades to me: for they transplant the Rose,
   And further South the Rose will bloom again
      Like a mere Rose that only cares for praise.

Note.—The last line suggests that the lament is for the departure
of some human rose from the Somersby district.

SONNET

I LINGERED yet awhile to bend my way
   To that far South, for which my spirits ache,
For under rainy hills a jewel lay
   And this dark land was precious for its sake,
   A rosy-coloured jewel, fit to make
An emperor's signet-ring, to save or slay
   Whole peoples, such as some great King might take
To clasp his mantle on a festal day:
And yet a jewel only made to shine,
   And icy cold although 'tis rosy clear—
      Why did I linger? I myself condemn,
For ah! 'tis far too costly to be mine,
   And nature never dropt a human tear
      In those chill dews whereof she froze the gem.

Note.—Tennyson in his youth had a great longing to go and live in some Mediterranean country, as his eldest brother, Frederick, did soon after leaving Cambridge. The sonnet is rather obscure, but I think the "Jewel" was human and feminine.

SONNET

W H E N that rank heat of evil's tropic day
   Made floating cloud of flowing joy, and cleft
My shores of life (their freshness steamed away,
   Nothing but salt and bitter crystals left),
When in my lonely walks I seemed to be
   An image of the cursed figtree, set
   In the brown glens of this Mount Olivet,
Thy looks, thy words, were sun and rain to me.
When all sin-sickened, loathing my disgrace,
   Far on within the temple of the mind
      I seemed to hear God speaking audibly,
"Let us go hence"—sometimes a little space,
   Out of the sphere of God, I dared to find
      A shadow and a resting place in thee.

Note.—This sonnet expresses a characteristic mood of depression and self-depreciation. Possibly the friend to whom it was addressed was Arthur Hallam.

SONNET

C O N R A D ! why call thy life monotonous?
    Why brood above thine anchor? the wov'n weed
    Calms not, but blackens, the slope water bed.
The shores of Life are fair and various,
    But thou dost ever by one beach abide.
Why hast thou drawn thine oars across the boat?
Thou canst not without impulse downward float,
    The wave of life hath no propelling tide.
We live but by *resistance*, and the best
    Of Life is but the struggle of the will:
    Thine unresisting boat shall pause—not still
But beaten on both sides by swaying Unrest.
Oh! cleave this calm to living eddies, breast
    This sloth-sprung weed with progress sensible.

MILTON'S MULBERRY

L o o k what love the puddle-pated squarecaps have
    for me!
I am Milton's mulberry, Milton's Milton's mulberry—
But they whip't and rusticated him who planted me,
Milton's Milton's mulberry, Milton's Milton's mul-
    berry.
Old and hollow, somewhat crooked in the shoulders as
    you see,
Full of summer foliage yet but propt and padded
    curiously,
I would sooner have been planted by the hand that
    planted me,
Than have grown in Paradise and dropped my fruit on
    Adam's knee—
Look what love the tiny-witted Trenchers have for me.

Note.—This poem, which is clearly of the Cambridge period,
refers, of course, to the mulberry tree at Christ's College, reported
to have been planted by the poet.

PART III
1830—1842

THE RUINED KILN

I

A M I L L I O N gossamers in field and fold
Were twinkling into green and gold,
Then basked the filmy stubbles warm and bare,
While thousands in a silent air
   Of dappled cloudlets roofed the day,
And sparrows in a jangling throng
Chirped all in one—a storm of song—
   As by the ruined kiln I lay.

II

All else like me, one peaceful presence kept,
On his bound sheaf October slept,
Thro' crumbling bricks the woolly thistle grew;
Yet in the round kiln slept the dew
   And, over harrowed glebe, was seen
Hard by one waning elm, the farm,
In tempered sunshine white and warm,
   Where Lucy lived the village-queen.

Note.—These lines occur in a small pocket-book, which is dated
in Hallam Tennyson's handwriting 1831–33, and I have found a
slightly different version written by Tennyson in ink in a proof
copy of the volume of 1832.

FRAGMENT

O V E R the dark world flies the wind
  And clatters in the sapless trees,
From cloud to cloud through darkness blind
  Quick stars scud o'er the sounding seas:
I look: the showery skirts unbind:
  Mars by the lonely Pleiades
Burns overhead: with brows declined
  I muse: I wander from my peace,
And still divide the rapid mind
  This way and that in search of ease.

Note.—This is from the same little pocket-book as the preceding lines. It is characteristic of Tennyson's nature poetry during the early "In Memoriam" period. MS. evidence suggests that many sections of that poem were founded on brief mood pictures like this, written in various metres.

BRITAIN

H A I L, Britain! In whatever zone
　　Binds the broad earth beneath the blue,
　　In ancient seasons or the new
No manlier front than thine is shewn.

Not for the wide sail-wandered tides
　　That ever round thee come and go,
　　The many ships of war that blow
The battle from their iron sides :

Not for a power that knows not check
　　To spread and float an ermined pall
　　Of Empire, from the ruin'd wall
Of royal Delhi to Quebec:

But that in righteousness thy power
　　Doth stand, thine Empire on thy word—
　　In thee no traitor voice is heard
Whatever danger threats the hour!

God keep thee strong as thou art free,
　　Free in the freedom of His law,
　　And brave all wrong to overawe,
Strong in the strength of unity.

Note.—The first version of these lines occurs as the beginning
of a long unpublished poem in a notebook which also contains some
stanzas of "The Two Voices"—finished in 1833. The copy from

L　　　　　73

which the stanzas are printed is in the handwriting of Emily Lady Tennyson, and evidently of a much later date. It is interesting to note that some other stanzas of the long poem were used, with slight adaptations, in "In Memoriam" (published 1850), the "Ode on the Death of the Duke of Wellington" (1852) and "Lines to the Marquis of Dufferin and Ava" (1889), forming in each case some of the most effective lines in the poem concerned.

(WHAT THOR SAID TO THE BARD BEFORE DINNER)

WHEREVER evil customs thicken
Break thro' with the hammer of iron rhyme,
  Till priest-craft and king-craft sicken,
But pap-meat-pamper not the time
  With the flock of the thunder-stricken.
If the world caterwaul, lay harder upon her
  Till she clapperclaw no longer,
  Bang thy stithy stronger and stronger,
Thy rhyme-hammer *shall* have honour.

Be not fairspoken neither stammer,
Nail her, knuckle her, thou swinge-buckler!
  Spare not: ribroast gaffer and gammer,
Be no shuffler, wear no muffler,
  But on thine anvil hammer and hammer!
If she call out lay harder upon her,
    This way and that nail
    Tag rag and bobtail,
Thy rhyme-hammer *shall* have honour.

On squire and parson, broker and banker,
Down let fall thine iron spanker,
  Spare not king or duke or critic,
Dealing out cross-buttock and flanker
  With thy clanging analytic!
If she call out lay harder upon her,

75

Stun her, stagger her,
Care not for swaggerer,
Thy rhyme-hammer *shall* have honour.

Note.—The first stanza is quoted by Hallam Tennyson in the
Memoir (Vol. I, p. 97) under date 1832.

SONNET

H o w thought you that this thing could captivate?
  What are those graces that could make her dear,
  Who is not worth the notice of a sneer
To rouse the vapid devil of her hate?
A speech conventional, so void of weight
  That after it has buzzed about one's ear,
  'Twere rich refreshment for a week to hear
The dentist babble or the barber prate;
A hand displayed with many a little art;
  An eye that glances on her neighbour's dress;
    A foot too often shewn for my regard;
An angel's form—a waiting-woman's heart;
  A perfect-featured face, expressionless,
    Insipid, as the Queen upon a card.

Note.—This sonnet is written on an old sheet of notepaper which contains also an early version of the "Bridesmaid" sonnet. This was written in 1836, so that the sonnet here printed evidently belongs to that date. The last line was used by the poet in "Aylmer's Field" (published 1864).

NEW YEAR'S EVE

LISTEN! bells in yonder town,
    Lin, lan, lone,
Over dale and over down,
    Lin, lan, lone,
Now the year is almost gone,
    Lin, lan, lone,
Dying, dying, almost gone,
    Lin, lan, lone,
Almost, almost, almost gone.

Listen how the bells begin,
    With a lin, lan, lin,
For the old year out and the new year in,
    With a lin-lan-lan and a lan-lan-lin,
And the old year out and the new year in,
    With a clash and a lin-lan-lin.

Put out the lights and let us go to bed,
The baby year is born, his father's dead,
And, settling back after that storm of sound,
From all the starry circle overhead
Hard silence drops upon the stony ground.

Note.—Cf. "The Mellow lin-lan-lone of Evening Bells" in
"Far-Far-Away"—published 1889.

AN IDLE RHYME

O H, what care I how many a fluke
   Sticks in the liver of the time?
I cannot prate against the Duke,
   I love to have an idle rhyme.

The muse would stumble from the tune,
   If I should ask her "Plump my purse,
Be for some popular forenoon
   The leading article in verse."

So gross a murmur in her ear
   Would make her dull as Davy's sow,
And with a sudden mildew sear
   The rathe fruitblossom on her brow.

For, though she has her hopes and fears,
   She dwells not on a single page,
But thrids the annals of the years,
   And runs her eye from age to age.

What's near is large to modern eyes,
   But disproportions fade away
Lower'd in the sleepy pits where lies
   The dropsied Epos of the day—

The day that rose like ours sublime
   In dreaming dreams and planning plans,
That thought herself the crown of time
   And took her many geese for swans.

Oh, so, when modern things are thrust
    By death below the coffin lid,
Our liberal sons will spurn our dust
    And wonder what it was we did—

However, you have spoken well,
    But, now the summer sun descends,
Unbroach that flask of cool Moselle
    And let us drink to all our friends.

But if you prate of "In" and "Out,"
    And Dan and Joe, whoe'er they be,
Then "οἴη φυλλων will I spout
    οἴη περ φυλλων γενεη."

As stretched beside the river clear
    That's round this glassy foreland curled,
I cool my face in flowers, and hear
    The deep pulsations of the world.

Note.—Style and mood suggest that this poem was written at about the same date as "The Talking Oak" and "Will Waterproof," both of which were published in 1842. The "Duke" is no doubt Wellington. By "Dan" and "Joe" are meant O'Connell and Hume. Cf. Sonnet on page 61.

The "Fluke" appears to be a parasitic worm that attacks the livers of sheep and other animals.

APPENDIX

CL. CLAUDIANI

DE RAPTU PROSERPINAE

(Book I. lines 1–93)

INFERNI raptoris equos, afflataque curru
Sidera Taenario, caligantesque profundae
Iunonis thalamos, audaci prodere cantu
Mens congesta jubet.   Gressus removete, profani.
Iam furor humanos nostro de pectore sensus
Expulit, et totum spirant praecordia Phoebum.
Iam mihi cernuntur trepidis delubra moveri
Sedibus, et claram dispergere culmina lucem,
Adventum testata Dei.   Iam magnus ab imis
Auditur fremitus terris, templumque remugit
Cecropium, sanctasque faces attollit Eleusin.
Angues Triptolemi stridunt, et squamea curvis
Colla levant attrita jugis, lapsuque sereno
Erecti roseas tendunt ad carmina cristas.
Ecce procul ternas Hecate variata figuras
Exoritur, lenisque simul procedit Iacchus
Crinali florens hedera, quem Parthica velat
Tigris, et auratos in nodum colligit ungues.
Ebria Maeonius firmat vestigia thyrsus.
    Di quibus in numerum vacui famulantur Averni
Vulgus iners, opibus quorum donatur avaris
Quicquid in orbe perit, quos Styx liventibus ambit

M   81

Interfusa vadis, et quos fumantia torquens
Aequora vorticibus Phlegethon perlustrat anhelis;
Vos mihi sacrarum penetralia pandite rerum,
Et vestri secreta poli: qua lampade Ditem
Flexit Amor, quo ducta ferox Proserpina raptu
Possedit dotale Chaos, quantasque per oras
Sollicito genetrix erraverit anxia cursu:
Unde datae populis leges, et glande relicta
Cesserit inventis Dodonia quercus aristis.
  Dux Erebi quondam tumidas exarsit in iras
Proelia moturus Superis, quod solus egeret
Connubii, sterilesque diu consumeret annos,
Impatiens nescire torum, nullasque mariti
Illecebras, nec dulce patris cognoscere nomen.
Iam quaecunque latent ferali monstra barathro
In turmas aciemque ruunt, contraque Tonantem
Conjurant Furiae: crinitaque sontibus hydris
Tisiphone, quatiens infausto lumine pinum,
Armatos ad castra vocat pallentia Manes.
Paene reluctatis iterum pugnantia rebus
Rupissent elementa fidem, penitusque revulso
Carcere, laxatis pubes Titania vinclis
Vidisset caeleste jubar, rursusque cruentus
Aegaeon positis arcto de corpore nodis
Obvia centeno vexasset fulmina motu.
Sed Parcae vetuere minas, orbique timentes
Ante pedes soliumque ducis fudere severam
Canitiem, genibusque suas cum supplice vultu
Admovere manus, quarum sub jure tenentur
Omnia, quae seriem fatorum pollice ducunt,
Longaque ferratis evolvunt secula pensis.
  Prima fero Lachesis clamabat talia regi,

Incultas dispersa comas: O maxime noctis
Arbiter, umbrarumque potens, cui nostra laborant
Stamina, qui finem cunctis et semina praebes,
Nascendique vices alterna morte rependis:
Qui vitam letumque regis: (nam quicquid ubique
Gignit materies, hoc te donante creatur,
Debeturque tibi, certisque ambagibus aevi
Rursus corporeos animae mittuntur in ortus:)
Ne pete firmatas pacis dissolvere leges,
Quas dedimus, nevitque colus: neu foedera fratrum
Civili converte tuba.   Cur impia tollis
Signa? quid incestis aperis Titanibus auras?
Posce Iovem, dabitur conjux. Vix illa: pepercit,
Erubuitque preces, animisque relanguit atrox,
Quamvis indocilis flecti.   Ceu turbine rauco
Cum gravis armatur Boreas, glacieque nivali
Hispidus, et Getica concretus grandine pennas
Bella cupit, pelagus, silvas, camposque sonoro
Flamine rapturus: si forte adversus aenos
Aeolus objecit postes, vanescit inanis
Impetus, et fractae redeunt in claustra procellae.
   Tum Maia genitum, qui fervida dicta reportet,
Imperat acciri.   Cyllenius adstitit ales,
Somniferam quatiens virgam, tectusque galero.
Ipse rudi fultus solio, nigraque verendus
Majestate sedet: squalent immania foedo
Sceptra situ: sublime caput maestissima nubes
Asperat, et dirae riget inclementia formae.
Terrorem dolor augebat.   Tunc talia celso
Ore tonat: (tremefacta silent dicente tyranno
Atria: latratum triplicem compescuit ingens
Ianitor, et presso lacrymarum fonte resedit

83

Cocytos, tacitisque Acheron obmutuit undis,
Et Phlegethonteae requierunt murmura ripae:)
   Atlantis Tegaee nepos, commune profundis
Et superis numen, qui fas per numen utrumque
Solus habes, geminoque facis commercia mundo,
I celeres proscinde Notos, et jussa superbo
Redde Iovi. Tantumne tibi, saevissime fratrum,
In me juris erit?